641·83
CRo

A 760 700 - 8
Jellinfield

D0512336

Sweet and savoury side dishes and main courses using the
freshest ingredients with imaginative and delicious dressings.

By the same author
THE SUBVERSIVE VEGETARIAN
(with Michael Cox)

SALADS

by

DESDA CROCKETT

Illustrated by Clive Birch

WELSH AGRICULTURAL
COLLEGE
JOINT LIBRARY
1 9 OCT 1984
ABERYSTWYTH COLLEGE
OF FURTHER EDUCATION

A THORSONS COOKBOOK
WHOLEFOOD

THORSONS PUBLISHERS LIMITED
Wellingborough, Northamptonshire

First published 1983

© DESDA CROCKETT 1983

This book is sold subject to the condition that it shall not, by way of trade or otherwise, be lent, re-sold, hired out, or otherwise circulated without the publisher's prior consent in any form of binding or cover other than that in which it is published and without a similar condition including this condition being imposed on the subsequent purchaser.

British Library Cataloguing in Publication Data

Crockett, Desda
    Salads.
    1. Vegetarianism   2. Salads
    641.8'3   TX807

    ISBN 0-7225-0764-X

Printed in Great Britain by
Richard Clay (The Chaucer Press) Ltd,
Bungay, Suffolk

CONTENTS

Wholefoods, quite simply, are foods in their natural state — nothing added, nothing taken away. In this age of mass-production foods, wholefoods are not always easy to obtain. But as nutritionists and doctors become increasingly convinced of their value in building and maintaining health, so their availability is fast improving.

Include as many natural, unadulterated foods as you can in your day to day eating pattern, and discover not just exciting new tastes and a fresh approach to mealtimes, but better health too.

INTRODUCTION

Ev'n in the spring and play-time of the year,
That calls th'unwonted villager abroad
With all her little ones, a sportive train,
To gather king-cups in the yellow mead,
And prink their hair with daisies, or to pick
A cheap but wholesome sallad from the brook,
These shades are all my own.

William Cowper, *The Task*, Book VI, 304

Cheap and wholesome — there in a nutshell is why salads are so invaluable, and so essential. Though nothing is cheap these days, salad ingredients remain excellent value for money and are available all the year round; they are also, one and all, good for you, providing necessary nutritional elements and natural goodness for all the family.

It has become something of a *cliché* to bemoan the awfulness of the traditional British salad, with its limited quota of ingredients (limp lettuce predominating); but though things are changing and people are slowly becoming aware of what a salad can be and do, all too often one encounters lack of imagination, poor presentation and sheer ignorance in relation to salads.

The salad is in fact an exceptionally versatile culinary art form, providing textures, colours and flavour combinations to excite the most jaded palate. Visually, it can be stunning; gastronomically, it can be second to none in the subtle orchestration of flavours and sensations the inspired combination of raw ingredients can provide.

The variety and excitement can be enjoyed throughout the year. Though we think of salads as mainly a summer way of eating, it could be argued that we actually need the nourishment they provide more during the winter months, when we are prone to become housebound and listless, than in the summer, when we get more fresh air and exercise.

In this book the recipes have been selected with the average family firmly in mind. Theoretically, the only limit with regard to salad combinations is your own imagination; but in practice the modern meal maker needs ideas that are quick and easy to prepare using ingredients that are readily obtainable from the local supermarket or corner grocery store.

Key Ingredients

The key to successful salad making is first of all to choose only the freshest, unblemished ingredients. Take especial care with lettuce and look carefully for any signs of browning or wilting (all wilted vegetables have lost considerable quantities of vitamin C).

If there are blemishes, remove them immediately, as well as all unwanted parts, such as the tops and tails of spring onions.

Wash *every* ingredient before use.

Lettuce: This remains the basic ingredient of many exquisite salads. There are three main types: cabbage (butterhead), iceberg and cos. Whichever type you prefer, always choose lettuces that look fresh, crisp and bright: never 'make do'.

Lettuces should *always* be handled gently because they bruise easily. The kid glove treatment should start when you buy your lettuce: don't stuff it into your bag — and don't let shop assistants handle lettuce roughly either.

Wash lettuce *quickly* in cold water before use. Pat it dry with a paper towel, or shake it dry in a salad basket. If you need to prepare your lettuce for a salad in advance of the meal, it can be wrapped (after washing) in a paper towel and left in the refrigerator for up to three hours — it will still retain its crispness.

Don't cut lettuce with a metal knife: whenever possible, tear it into small pieces.

Cucumber: Choose cucumbers that are straight and firm to the touch — about two inches is the best width.

If you prefer your cucumber peeled, cut it in half and peel the skin back to within about half an inch of each end (the blossom end of a cucumber can often be bitter). In general, though, try leaving the skin on the cucumber. For an attractive effect, score the cucumber lengthways with a fork before slicing.

If you grow your own cucumbers, remember that the flowers can also be eaten raw; alternatively, they can be fried in batter.

To reduce the water content of cucumbers, sprinkle the slices with salt and leave them for about thirty minutes in a colander. Rinse off the salt and dry the cucumber before use.

Tomatoes: For most salads, leave the skins on tomatoes. If you need them peeled, prick the skins with the tip of a knife and plunge them into boiling water. After about a minute, lift them out and plunge them immediately into cold water, after which the skins will peel off easily.

When buying tomatoes, make sure they are firm and regular in shape. The colour should be bright, with no blotches or cracks, and the skin should have a matt texture.

Basic salad vegetables: As well as the foregoing, use the following ingredients freely as they become available: artichokes, asparagus, avocados, basil, beans (broad beans, French beans, kidney beans, runner beans), beetroot (fresh), cabbage (white and red as well as the green varieties), carrots (grated), cauliflower, celeriac, celery, chard, chicory, chives, coriander leaves, endive, fennel, kohlrabi, mushrooms, nasturtium leaves, onions (especially spring onions), parsley, peas, peppers (red and green), potatoes, radishes, salsify leaves, watercress.

Garlic: I list this as a key ingredient out of personal preference, but if you find the regular use of garlic to be unacceptable it is enough to rub the cut edge of a garlic clove around the inside of your salad bowl before the salad is tossed.

The French use a piece of bread called a *chapon* that has been rubbed with garlic and with which the salad is tossed. The bread is removed before serving, leaving behind only a slight garlic flavour. It is best to use stale bread for this purpose.

Nuts: Whole, chopped or toasted, nuts can add interest, texture and protein to many salads. They can be used either as a main ingredient or as a garnish.

Dressings

Never use malt vinegar: apart from any other considerations, it is too harsh and heavy. Cider vinegar is better on every count and has positive health benefits.

You can also use wine vinegars (red or white) or buy unflavoured wine vinegars and add your own flavourings with freshly picked or dried herbs.

Whatever dressing is being used, pour it over your salad at the last possible moment.

For many salads, a simple vinaigrette dressing consisting of equal parts of oil and vinegar (or lemon) is best. Use either olive oil, sunflower oil or a mixture of the two, as olive oil is becoming prohibitively expensive.

Never insult your salad by deluging it in commercial salad cream.

BASIC FRENCH DRESSING

Imperial (Metric)	American
6 tablespoonsful olive or sunflower oil	7½ tablespoonsful olive or sunflower oil
2 tablespoonsful cider or wine vinegar	2½ tablespoonsful cider or wine vinegar
1 teaspoonful sea salt	1 teaspoonful sea salt
1 teaspoonful freshly ground black pepper	1 teaspoonful freshly ground black pepper
½ teaspoonful raw cane sugar	½ teaspoonful raw cane sugar
½ clove garlic, crushed	½ clove garlic, crushed
½ teaspoonful ready-made Meaux mustard	½ teaspoonful ready-made Meaux mustard

Put all the ingredients in a screw-topped jam jar. Shake vigorously until all the ingredients are thoroughly mixed. This can be kept in the refrigerator and used as required.

HONEY AND VINEGAR DRESSING

Imperial (Metric)	American
1 teaspoonful chives	1 teaspoonful chives
¼ pint (150ml) cider vinegar	⅔ cupful cider vinegar
1 tablespoonful clear honey	1 tablespoonful clear honey
Seasoning to taste	Seasoning to taste

Chop the chives finely. Place them with the rest of the ingredients in a jam jar and shake well. Use as required.

YOGURT DRESSING

Imperial (Metric)	American
½ pint (¼ litre) natural yogurt	1⅓ cupsful natural yogurt
4 tablespoonsful lemon juice	5 tablespoonsful lemon juice
1 teaspoonful sea salt	1 teaspoonful sea salt
1 teaspoonful freshly ground black pepper	1 teaspoonful freshly ground black pepper
1 clove garlic, crushed	1 clove garlic, crushed

Beat the ingredients together in a bowl until they are thoroughly mixed. Use this dressing immediately.

MAYONNAISE

Imperial (Metric)	American
1 egg yolk	1 egg yolk
¼ teaspoonful dry mustard	¼ teaspoonful dry mustard
Seasoning to taste	Seasoning to taste
Pinch of raw cane sugar	Pinch of raw cane sugar
2 tablespoonsful cider or wine vinegar	2½ tablespoonsful cider or wine vinegar
¼ pint (150ml) olive or sunflower oil	⅔ cupful olive or sunflower oil

Place the egg yolk, dry mustard, seasoning and sugar in a mixing bowl and beat until the ingredients are well combined and thickened. Add the vinegar and whisk with a wooden spoon until frothy. Add the oil drop by drop, whisking as you do so. Be careful not to add the oil too quickly or the mixture will curdle.

BLUE CHEESE DRESSING

Imperial (Metric)
Approx. ¼ pint (100-150ml)
    mayonnaise (page 14)
4 oz (100g) blue cheese (Danish
    blue, Stilton, etc.)
Approx. ¼ pint (100-150ml) double
    cream
Seasoning to taste

American
Approx. ⅔ cupful mayonnaise
    (page 14)
4 oz blue cheese (Danish blue,
    Stilton, etc.)
Approx. ⅔ cupful heavy cream
Seasoning to taste

Beat all the ingredients together thoroughly in a mixing bowl. Store in the refrigerator and use as required.

LOW CALORIE DRESSING

Imperial (Metric)
6 spring onions
1 clove garlic, crushed
2 tablespoonsful fresh lemon juice
½ lb (¼ kilo) cottage cheese
Approx. ¼ pint (125-150ml) milk
Seasoning to taste

American
6 scallions
1 clove garlic, crushed
2½ tablespoonsful fresh lemon juice
1 cupful cottage cheese
Approx. ⅔ cupful milk
Seasoning to taste

Chop the spring onions and combine them with all the other ingredients in a mixing bowl. Mix well and chill before use.

TOMATO JUICE DRESSING

Imperial (Metric)
½ pint (¼ litre) fresh tomato juice
1 tablespoonful cider vinegar
1 clove garlic, crushed
Seasoning to taste

American
1⅓ cupsful fresh tomato juice
1 tablespoonful cider vinegar
1 clove garlic, crushed
Seasoning to taste

Combine all the ingredients in a screw-topped jar. Season to taste, shake well and chill before serving.

THOUSAND ISLAND DRESSING

Imperial (Metric)
¾ pint (400ml) mayonnaise
  (page 14)
1 teaspoonful Tabasco sauce
2 tablespoonsful sweet pickle
10 stuffed green olives, chopped
2 hard-boiled eggs, finely chopped
1 small onion, finely chopped
3 tablespoonsful olive oil
1 tablespoonful cider vinegar
Seasoning to taste

American
2 cupsful mayonnaise
  (page 14)
1 teaspoonful Tabasco sauce
2½ tablespoonsful sweet pickle
10 stuffed green olives, chopped
2 hard-boiled eggs, finely chopped
1 small onion, finely chopped
3½ tablespoonsful olive oil
1 tablespoonful cider vinegar
Seasoning to taste

Mix all the ingredients thoroughly and chill the dressing well before serving.

CURRY MAYONNAISE

Imperial (Metric)	American
4 tablespoonsful mayonnaise (page 14)	5 tablespoonsful mayonnaise (page 14)
¼ pint (150ml) natural yogurt	⅔ cupful natural yogurt
2 teaspoonsful curry paste	2 teaspoonsful curry paste
1 tablespoonful lemon juice	1 tablespoonful lemon juice
Seasoning to taste	Seasoning to taste

Mix all the ingredients together until smooth and creamy.

CHINESE SOY DRESSING

Imperial (Metric)	American
1½ tablespoonsful soy sauce	1½ tablespoonsful soy sauce
1 tablespoonful clear honey	1 tablespoonful clear honey
1 tablespoonful sunflower oil	1 tablespoonful sunflower oil
1 teaspoonful dried ground ginger	1 teaspoonful dried ground ginger
2 tablespoonsful lemon juice	2½ tablespoonsful lemon juice
2 pinches of cayenne pepper	2 pinches of cayenne pepper

Mix all the ingredients together thoroughly.

Sprouting

Sprouted seeds are amongst the most nutritious foods in the world. They are rich in vitamins (particularly vitamin C) and minerals (for example, calcium, potassium, iron and iodine). They also contain enzymes, which we need to control many of the complex chemical reactions that take place in our bodies. The vitamin content increases as the seeds begin to sprout: from a dry state, some bean sprouts show an increase in vitamin C of several hundred per cent after only three days.

Only buy seed that is intended for sprouting: seed that is intended for sowing will almost certainly have been treated with some sort of chemical dressing. Store your seed in a cool, dry place away from the light and in air-tight jars.

Before sprouting, pick out damaged or discoloured seeds and any foreign bodies. There are several sprouting methods and it is worth experimenting to get the best results.* One simple method is as follows:

1. Put a layer of seeds (about ¼ in./5mm) in the bottom of a jam jar.

2. Run some cold water into the jar, shake the seeds around and drain off the water. This can be done by placing a piece of fine muslin over the top of the jar, secured with an elastic band. (You may need to replace the muslin quite often as it tends to discolour.)

3. Place the jar on a window-sill or, better, in an airing cupboard.

4. Morning and evening, run more cold water into the jar, swirl the seeds round and drain off the excess water. The seeds may grow so rapidly that you have to transfer some of them to another jar. (Remember that sprouted seeds always need to be kept moist.)

*A good selection of methods, together with recipes, is given in *The Complete Sprouting Book* by Per and Gita Sellmann (Turnstone Press, 1981).

If you prefer, there are several specially designed sprouters on the market, usually with two or three layers so that several types of seed can be sprouted at once.

Seeds must be harvested when they reach their optimum size (which varies from one kind to another) and must never be over-grown. About four days is the average time it takes for sprouts to become ready for harvesting. Once they are harvested they can be kept for two or three days in the refrigerator. Rinsing them occasionally with cold water helps keep them fresh.

Amongst the most commonly sprouted seeds are: aduki beans, alfalfa, fenugreek, chick peas, lentils, mung beans, soya beans; cereals (barley, wheat, rye); sunflower seeds and mustard and cress.

Herbs

Try to include herbs in your salads as often as possible. They add interest, colour, texture and piquancy to any salad combination and many have medicinal properties that have been recognized for centuries. The use of herbs for garnishing also helps to reduce the need for additional salt or pepper.

You can, of course, keep a rack in the kitchen stocked with the packaged dried herbs that are now widely available, but for those who wish to make the very best possible use of herbs it is far better to grow what you need. You can grow parsley easily in a pot on the kitchen window-sill, and many other herbs can be grown in shallow pots indoors. For those with gardens there is no need to create a special herb garden: simply plant your herbs (either from seed or pot-grown) in any and every available gap. Some varieties, like borage, are quite happy growing in a gravel drive.

For salad making the following are always useful: parsley, chives, dill, basil, fennel, borage, lemon balm, mint, thyme, rosemary, chervil, caraway and lovage.

Nutritional Benefits

Salad ingredients, like all raw, unprocessed foods, are living sub-stances and a primary source of the vitamins, minerals and trace elements our bodies need, in a form we can assimilate easily and naturally. A salad a day is the ideal way of providing you and your family with the nutritional benefits of raw food, but eating a well prepared salad just two or three times a week will go a long way to ensuring the provision of essential nutrients. The accompanying table indicates just some of the nutritional elements to be found in common salad ingredients.

Note: In all the recipes, quantities are for *four* people. 'Seasoning' means the sparing addition of *sea salt* and *freshly ground black pepper*.

Some Nutritional Elements in Common Salad Ingredients (based on 4oz/100g serving)

Food	Protein (g)	Carbohydrate (g)	Calcium (mg)	Iron (mg)	Vitamin A (IU)	Vitamin B₁ (mg)	Vitamin C (mg)	Calories
Almonds	18.6	19.5	234	4.7	—	.24	trace	598
Apple	.2	14.5	7	.3	90	.03	4	58
Banana	1.1	22.2	8	.7	190	.05	10	85
Brazil nuts	14.3	10.9	186	3.4	trace	.96	—	654
Cabbage	1.3	5.4	49	.4	130	.05	47	24
Carrots	1.1	9.7	37	.7	11,000	.06	8	42
Celery	.9	3.9	39	.3	240	.03	9	17
Cucumber	.9	3.4	25	1.1	250	.03	11	15
Garlic	6.2	30.8	29	1.5	trace	.25	15	137
Grapes	1.3	15.7	16	.4	100	.05	4	69
Kale	6.0	9.0	249	2.7	10,000	.16	186	53
Lettuce	.9	2.9	20	.5	330	.06	6	13
Onions	1.5	8.7	27	.5	40	.03	10	38
Pears	.7	15.3	8	.3	20	.02	4	61
Peppers	1.2	4.8	9	.7	420	.08	128	22
Potatoes	2.1	17.1	7	.6	trace	.10	20	76
Radishes	1.0	3.6	30	1.0	10	.03	26	17
Strawberries	.7	8.4	21	1.0	30	.03	59	37
Tomatoes	1.1	4.7	13	.5	900	.06	28	22
Walnuts	14.8	15.8	99	3.1	30	.33	2	651

1.

SIDE SALADS AND STARTERS

BASIC GREEN SALAD

Imperial (Metric)
½ lettuce, separated into leaves and torn
½ bunch watercress
¼ bunch curly endive (if available)
1 green pepper, de-seeded and thinly sliced
Thin slices of cucumber
Spring onions
French dressing (page 13)
Chopped parsley

American
½ lettuce, separated into leaves and torn
½ bunch watercress
¼ bunch curly endive (if available)
1 green pepper, de-seeded and thinly sliced
Thin slices of cucumber
Scallions
French dressing (page 13)
Chopped parsley

1. Place all the vegetables except the parsley in a deep salad bowl.

2. Just before serving, pour over the dressing and toss well.

3. Garnish with freshly chopped parsley.

There are many variations on the basic green salad. Any of the following can be included:

Raw spinach Tear leaves to the size required.
Avocado slices Toss in lemon juice to prevent them from going brown.
Fresh herbs Chop finely — e.g. mint, borage, dill, fennel.
Olives Whole or sliced.
Chicory Sliced thinly or tear the leaves.

BEANSPROUT SALAD

Imperial (Metric)
½ lb (¼ kilo) fresh beansprouts
1 small red pepper, chopped
2 small spring onions, chopped
1 pickled cucumber, diced
1 oz (25g) blanched almond flakes

American
4 cupsful fresh beansprouts
1 small red pepper, chopped
2 small scallions, chopped
1 pickled cucumber, diced
¼ cupful blanched almond flakes

Dressing:

Imperial (Metric)
2 teaspoonsful soy sauce
1 teaspoonful dry sherry
2 tablespoonsful olive or sunflower oil
1 dessertspoonful cider vinegar
½ teaspoonful raw cane sugar
½ teaspoonful sea salt
½ teaspoonful prepared mustard
Pinch of ground ginger
Freshly ground black pepper

American
2 teaspoonsful soy sauce
1 teaspoonful dry sherry
2½ tablespoonsful olive or sunflower oil
1 tablespoonful cider vinegar
½ teaspoonful raw cane sugar
½ teaspoonful sea salt
½ teaspoonful prepared mustard
Pinch of ground ginger
Freshly ground black pepper

1. Put the beansprouts into a salad bowl with the red pepper, spring onions, cucumber and almond flakes.

2. In a jam jar, mix together all the ingredients for the dressing and shake them well until thoroughly combined.

3. Pour the dressing over the salad and chill well before serving.

BEETROOT AND YOGURT SALAD

Imperial (Metric)	American
4 beetroots	4 beetroots
½ pint (¼ litre) natural yogurt	1⅓ cupsful natural yogurt
2 cloves garlic, crushed	2 cloves garlic, crushed
Seasoning to taste	Seasoning to taste
½ teaspoonful caraway seeds	½ teaspoonful caraway seeds
Paprika	Paprika

1. Boil or bake the beetroots until tender. Allow them to cool and rub off the skins carefully, then dice them and arrange them in a dish.

2. Beat the yogurt with the garlic, seasoning and caraway seeds. Pour this over the beetroot and garnish with the paprika.

BROAD BEAN SALAD

Imperial (Metric)	American
1 lb (½ kilo) young broad beans	1 lb young Windsor beans
1 teaspoonful lemon juice	1 teaspoonful lemon juice
2 tablespoonsful olive oil	2½ tablespoonsful olive oil
1 clove garlic, crushed	1 clove garlic, crushed
Seasoning to taste	Seasoning to taste
2 tablespoonsful sour cream	2½ tablespoonsful sour cream
1 tablespoonful chopped chives or parsley	1 tablespoonful chopped chives or parsley

1. Top and tail the bean pods and remove the beans.

2. Slice the pods into very thin strips and put these and the beans into a bowl. Cover with boiling water and leave them for about 1 minute, then drain.

3. Mix together the lemon juice, oil, garlic and seasoning.

4. Put the beans and pods into a serving bowl and pour the dressing over them. Leave to marinade for about an hour.

5. Mix the sour cream and parsley or chives and pour this over the beans. Mix thoroughly.

CABBAGE SALAD

Imperial (Metric)	American
½ lb (¼ kilo) red cabbage	½ lb red cabbage
½ lb (¼ kilo) white cabbage	½ lb white cabbage
1 small onion	1 small onion
1 green pepper	1 green pepper
4 tablespoonsful sunflower oil	5 tablespoonsful sunflower oil
2 tablespoonsful cider vinegar	2½ tablespoonsful cider vinegar
Seasoning to taste	Seasoning to taste
Chopped parsley to garnish	Chopped parsley to garnish

1. Shred the red and the white cabbage very thinly and put into a bowl.

2. Peel the onion and slice it into thin rings. De-seed the pepper and cut it into thin strips. Add to the cabbage, season, and mix gently.

3. Mix the oil, vinegar and seasoning in a jar and shake them well.

4. Pour the dressing over the salad, toss gently and chill well. Garnish with the parsley.

CELERIAC SALAD

Imperial (Metric)
1 large celeriac
½ teaspoonful French mustard
3 tablespoonsful mayonnaise
　(page 14)

American
1 large celeriac
½ teaspoonful French mustard
3½ tablespoonsful mayonnaise
　(page 14)

1.　Peel the celeriac, cut it into thin slices and then into matchstick-sized pieces.

2.　Cook the celeriac in boiling salted water for about 3 minutes, then drain and allow it to cool.

3.　Blend the French mustard and the mayonnaise in a salad bowl, add the cooked celeriac and mix it in thoroughly. Chill before serving.

CELERY AND BEETROOT SALAD

Imperial (Metric)	American
1 large beetroot, cooked	1 large beet, cooked
½ head celery	½ head celery
1 teaspoonful raw cane sugar	1 teaspoonful raw cane sugar
3 tablespoonsful sunflower oil	3½ tablespoonsful sunflower oil
2 tablespoonsful cider vinegar	2½ tablespoonsful cider vinegar
1 medium-sized onion, chopped	1 medium-sized onion, chopped

1. Peel the beetroot and cut it into narrow strips about 2 in. long.

2. Wash the celery and cut it into 2-in. lengths.

3. Make a dressing with the sugar, oil and vinegar.

4. Arrange the onion, celery and beetroot on a dish and pour the dressing over them.

CHAMPIGNONS À LA CRÈME

Imperial (Metric)	American
1½ lb (¾ kilo) button mushrooms	1½ lb button mushrooms
4 oz (100g) butter	½ cupful butter
Strained juice of 1 lemon	Strained juice of 1 lemon
1 clove garlic, crushed	1 clove garlic, crushed

Dressing:

Imperial (Metric)	American
2 oz (50g) butter	¼ cupful butter
1 tablespoonful wholemeal flour	1 tablespoonful wholemeal flour
¼ pint (150ml) milk	⅔ cupful milk
Seasoning to taste	Seasoning to taste
2 tablespoonsful single cream	2½ tablespoonsful single cream
Chopped fresh parsley	Chopped fresh parsley

1. Wash the mushrooms and trim the stalks, then pat them dry.

2. Melt the 4 oz (100g) of butter in a saucepan and add the lemon juice. Stir in the mushrooms and garlic and cook them gently for about 4 minutes.

3. In another saucepan, melt the 2 oz (50g) of butter. Stir in the flour, and add the milk and seasoning. Stir well over a low heat for about 8 minutes, then remove the pan from the heat and stir in the cream.

4. Put the mushrooms into a serving bowl. Pour the dressing over them and chill well. Garnish with chopped parsley before serving.

CHOPPED PARSLEY SALAD

Imperial (Metric)	American
2 oz (50g) parsley, chopped	2 cupsful chopped parsley
2 tablespoonsful sunflower oil	2½ tablespoonsful sunflower oil
1 tablespoonful lemon juice	1 tablespoonful lemon juice
Freshly ground black pepper	Freshly ground black pepper

1. Put the parsley into a small salad bowl.

2. Add the oil and lemon juice and pepper to taste. Mix gently and serve immediately with cream or cottage cheese.

COLE-SLAW

Imperial (Metric)	American
1 medium-sized onion	1 medium-sized onion
1 lb (½ kilo) white cabbage	1 lb white cabbage
Seasoning to taste	Seasoning to taste
2 tablespoonsful cider vinegar	2½ tablespoonsful cider vinegar
½ teaspoonful raw cane sugar	½ teaspoonful raw cane sugar
3 tablespoonsful mayonnaise (page 14)	3½ tablespoonsful mayonnaise (page 14)
Chopped parsley	Chopped parsley

1. Peel the onion and grate it coarsely. Grate the cabbage and put it with the onion in a deep bowl.

2. Sprinkle the cabbage and onion with the seasoning and pour the vinegar and sugar over them, then spoon in the mayonnaise.

3. Mix thoroughly and garnish with parsley.

CONTINENTAL POTATO SALAD

Imperial (Metric)	American
1 lb (½ kilo) cooked potatoes	1 lb cooked potatoes
1 small onion	1 small onion
3 gherkins	3 gherkins
1 teaspoonful capers	1 teaspoonful capers
1 teaspoonful chopped chives	1 teaspoonful chopped chives
¼ pint (150ml) natural yogurt	⅔ cupful natural yogurt
4 tablespoonsful mayonnaise (page 14)	5 tablespoonsful mayonnaise (page 14)
3 tablespoonsful cider vinegar	3½ tablespoonsful cider vinegar
2 tablespoonsful olive oil	2½ tablespoonsful olive oil
1 teaspoonful raw cane sugar	1 teaspoonful raw cane sugar
Seasoning to taste	Seasoning to taste
1 teaspoonful chopped fresh parsley	1 teaspoonful chopped fresh parsley

1. Cut the peeled potatoes into thin slices.

2. Chop the onion, gherkins, capers and chives finely.

3. Mix the yogurt with the mayonnaise, chives, vinegar, oil, gherkins, capers and sugar and season well.

4. Spoon the mixture over the potatoes and mix it in carefully.

5. Garnish with parsley.

CRISPY SPROUT SALAD

Imperial (Metric)	American
4 oz (100g) beansprouts	2 cupsful beansprouts
1 punnet of cress	1 punnet of cress
1 small carrot	1 small carrot
¼ red cabbage	¼ red cabbage
½ red pepper	½ red pepper

1. Wash and drain the beansprouts and place them in a shallow bowl. Cut and wash the cress and drain it.

2. Peel and cut the carrot into thin strips.

3. Slice the red cabbage finely, then de-seed and chop the pepper finely.

4. Put the cabbage, pepper, cress and carrot in a bowl with the sprouts and mix them together gently.

Note: This can be served with a vinaigrette dressing (page 12), but also makes a very colourful and tasty salad on its own.

CUCUMBER SALAD

Imperial (Metric)	American
1 cucumber	1 cucumber
4 spring onions or 1 medium-sized onion	4 scallions or 1 medium-sized onion
2 tablespoonsful sunflower oil	2½ tablespoonsful sunflower oil
2 tablespoonsful cider vinegar	2½ tablespoonsful cider vinegar
Seasoning to taste	Seasoning to taste
1 clove garlic, crushed	1 clove garlic, crushed
1 tablespoonful double cream	1 tablespoonful heavy cream
½ teaspoonful dried dill	½ teaspoonful dried dill

1. Peel the cucumber and slice it very thinly. Place the slices in a sieve and leave them to drain for about 30 minutes. Pat dry with a paper towel.

2. Chop the onions finely.

3. In a bowl, whisk the oil, vinegar, seasoning, garlic, cream and dill.

4. Lay the sliced cucumber in a salad bowl and pour the dressing over the top. Garnish with the chopped onions.

Note: If you are in a hurry, there is no need to drain the cucumber. Just add the dressing when the cucumber is sliced.

FENNEL SALAD

Imperial (Metric)
3 medium-sized fennel heads
1 medium-sized eating apple
2 spring onions or 1 medium-sized
  onion
2 or 3 radishes
French dressing (page 13)

American
3 medium-sized fennel heads
1 medium-sized eating apple
2 scallions or 1 medium-sized
  onion
2 or 3 radishes
French dressing (page 13)

1. Wash and chop the fennel.

2. Core (but do not peel) and slice the apple.

3. Chop the spring onions and slice the radishes, then place them in a salad bowl with the fennel and apple.

4. Pour over the dressing and toss the salad gently. Chill well before serving.

FRENCH BEAN SALAD

Imperial (Metric)	American
1 lb (½ kilo) young French beans	1 lb young snap beans
6 tablespoonsful olive oil	7½ tablespoonsful olive oil
2 tablespoonsful lemon juice	2½ tablespoonsful lemon juice
½ clove garlic, crushed	½ clove garlic, crushed
Seasoning to taste	Seasoning to taste
1 hard-boiled egg	1 hard-boiled egg

1. Cook the beans in boiling salted water for about 8 minutes. Drain and arrange them on a round dish to form a star shape.

2. Mix the oil, lemon juice, garlic and seasoning and pour the dressing over the beans. Allow the salad to cool.

3. Separate the white from the yolk of the egg. Rub the yolk through a coarse sieve and chop the white finely.

4. Place the chopped egg white in the centre of the beans and garnish the whole salad with the sieved yolk. Chill well before serving.

GERMAN POTATO SALAD

Imperial (Metric)	American
1 lb (½ kilo) small new potatoes	1 lb small new potatoes
2 tablespoonsful cider vinegar	2½ tablespoonsful cider vinegar
½ teaspoonful raw cane sugar	½ teaspoonful raw cane sugar
Seasoning to taste	Seasoning to taste
1 small onion	1 small onion
1 tablespoonful chopped gherkins	1 tablespoonful chopped gherkins
4 tablespoonsful mayonnaise (page 14)	5 tablespoonsful mayonnaise (page 14)
1 hard-boiled egg	1 hard-boiled egg
Chopped fresh parsley	Chopped fresh parsley

1. Wash the potatoes well, but leave the skins on. Boil them in salted water until tender, then drain them and leave them to cool.

2. Put the cider vinegar, sugar and seasoning into a serving bowl and mix them thoroughly.

3. Skin and slice the cooled potatoes thinly, then peel and chop the onion and place them in a bowl with the dressing and the gherkins.

4. Add the mayonnaise and mix it in thoroughly.

5. Cut the hard-boiled egg into wedges and arrange it on top of the potato mixture. Garnish with the chopped parsley and chill well before serving.

GREEN PEPPER SALAD

Imperial (Metric)	American
4 green peppers	4 green peppers
1 red pepper	1 red pepper
1 clove garlic, crushed	1 clove garlic, crushed
¼ teaspoonful sea salt	¼ teaspoonful sea salt
5 tablespoonsful olive oil	6 tablespoonsful olive oil
Black olives	Black olives

1. Skin the peppers by scorching them over a flame until the skin turns black, then scrape the skin off with a knife.

2. Quarter the skinned peppers, remove the seeds and cut them into strips. Arrange them on a large serving plate.

3. Put the garlic in a bowl and crush in the salt until almost liquid. Using a wire whisk, gradually add the olive oil and beat it in well.

4. Pour the garlic dressing over the peppers and garnish with the olives. Chill well before serving.

GREEK CUCUMBER AND YOGURT SALAD

Imperial (Metric)	American
1 cucumber	1 cucumber
1 tablespoonful sea salt	1 tablespoonful sea salt
2 cloves garlic	2 cloves garlic
2 teaspoonsful dried mint or 2 tablespoonsful chopped fresh mint	2 teaspoonsful dried mint or 2 tablespoonsful chopped fresh mint
1 tablespoonful lemon juice	1 tablespoonful lemon juice
1 pint (½ litre) natural yogurt	2½ cupsful natural yogurt
1 tablespoonful double cream	1 tablespoonful heavy cream
Seasoning to taste	Seasoning to taste

1. Peel and dice the cucumber and place it in a colander. Sprinkle the cucumber with the sea salt and leave it to drain, covered with a plate, for about an hour.

2. Crush the garlic with a little salt until creamy. Mix it in a bowl with the mint and lemon juice. Beat in the yogurt and cream.

3. Dry the cucumber on kitchen paper and place it in a bowl.

4. Pour over the dressing and season. Garnish with fresh mint if available. Chill well before serving.

JERUSALEM ARTICHOKE SALAD

Imperial (Metric)	American
1 lb (½ kilo) Jerusalem artichokes	1 lb Jerusalem artichokes
2 teaspoonsful lemon juice	2 teaspoonsful lemon juice
3 tablespoonsful olive oil	3½ tablespoonsful olive oil
1 clove garlic, crushed	1 clove garlic, crushed
Seasoning to taste	Seasoning to taste
Chopped parsley	Chopped parsley

1. Wash, peel and cook the artichokes for about 15 minutes, until just tender, then drain them.

2. Make a dressing with the lemon juice, oil, garlic and seasoning.

3. Put the artichokes into a serving bowl, cover them with the dressing and leave them for about half an hour. Garnish them with parsley before serving.

KOHLRABI SALAD

Imperial (Metric)	American
2 small kohlrabi	2 small kohlrabi
2 hard-boiled egg yolks	2 hard-boiled egg yolks
¼ pint (150ml) natural yogurt	⅔ cupful natural yogurt
¼ pint (150ml) mayonnaise (page 14)	⅔ cupful mayonnaise (page 14)
1 teaspoonful French mustard	1 teaspoonful French mustard
1 tablespoonful chopped dill	1 tablespoonful chopped dill
1 tablespoonful chopped chives	1 tablespoonful chopped chives
1 tablespoonful chopped parsley	1 tablespoonful chopped parsley
Seasoning to taste	Seasoning to taste

1. Peel the kohlrabi and grate it finely, then place it in a salad bowl.

2. Mash the hard-boiled egg yolks.

3. Mix the yogurt and mayonnaise until smooth, then add the egg yolks and mustard and mix again. Stir in the chopped herbs and seasoning.

4. Spoon this mixture over the kohlrabi and mix it in thoroughly. Chill and serve.

MARROW MAYONNAISE

Imperial (Metric)	American
1 medium-sized marrow	1 medium-sized summer squash
3 teaspoonsful raw cane sugar	3 teaspoonsful raw cane sugar
3 teaspoonsful lemon juice	3 teaspoonsful lemon juice
Sea salt to taste	Sea salt to taste
3 tablespoonsful mayonnaise (page 14)	3½ tablespoonsful mayonnaise (page 14)
1 tablespoonful chopped mixed fresh herbs	1 tablespoonful chopped mixed fresh herbs

1. Peel the marrow and remove the pulp. Shred the marrow on a coarse grater.

2. Place the marrow in a deep bowl and mix it well with all the other ingredients.

Note: Courgettes (zucchinis) may also be used.

MEXICAN TOMATO SALAD

Imperial (Metric)	American
1 small cucumber	1 small cucumber
5 spring onions, chopped	5 scallions, chopped
1 green pepper	1 green pepper
3 tomatoes	3 tomatoes
¼ pint (150ml) olive oil	⅔ cupful olive oil
5 tablespoonsful white wine vinegar	6 tablespoonsful white wine vinegar
1 clove garlic, crushed	1 clove garlic, crushed
1 teaspoonful dried basil	1 teaspoonful dried basil
Seasoning to taste	Seasoning to taste
½ lb (¼ kilo) button mushrooms	4 cupsful button mushrooms
5 tablespoonsful chopped parsley	6 tablespoonsful chopped parsley

1. Peel the cucumber and slice it thinly.

2. Place the slices of cucumber in a colander, sprinkle them with a little sea salt and leave them to drain for about 15 minutes. Rinse them with cold water and pat dry with kitchen paper. Place the cucumber in a large bowl with the spring onions.

3. Quarter, de-seed and cut the pepper into strips. Cut the tomatoes into wedges and put them in the bowl with the cucumber and onion.

4. Make the dressing by mixing together the oil, vinegar, garlic, basil and seasoning in a jam jar. Shake thoroughly.

5. Wash and dry the button mushrooms and put them whole into the bowl with the other ingredients. Pour the dressing over the top and mix it in gently. Chill for about an hour and garnish with parsley before serving.

MIXED ROOT VEGETABLE SALAD

Imperial (Metric)	American
2 small carrots	2 small carrots
1 parsnip	1 parsnip
1 small swede	1 small rutabaga
1 medium-sized raw beetroot	1 medium-sized raw beet
1 small onion	1 small onion
4 tablespoonsful sunflower oil	5 tablespoonsful sunflower oil
2 teaspoonsful raw cane sugar	2 teaspoonsful raw cane sugar
3 tablespoonsful pure lemon juice	3½ tablespoonsful pure lemon juice
2 teaspoonsful chopped fresh parsley	2 teaspoonsful chopped fresh parsley
Seasoning to taste	Seasoning to taste

1. Wash and peel all the vegetables and grate them finely, then mix them together in a bowl.

2. Make a dressing with the oil, sugar, lemon juice, parsley and seasoning and pour it over the vegetables, mixing well.

MUSHROOMS À LA GRECQUE

Imperial (Metric)	American
1½ lb (¾ kilo) button mushrooms	1½ lb button mushrooms
1 small onion	1 small onion
1 clove garlic	1 clove garlic
½ pint (150ml) wine vinegar	1⅓ cupsful wine vinegar
Juice of 1 small lemon	Juice of 1 small lemon
2 tablespoonsful raw cane sugar	2½ tablespoonsful raw cane sugar
Sprig of parsley	Sprig of parsley
1 bouquet garni	1 bouquet garni
Seasoning to taste	Seasoning to taste
Chopped fresh parsley	Chopped fresh parsley

1. Wash the mushrooms and remove the stalks.

2. Peel and chop the onion and garlic finely.

3. Bring the vinegar, lemon juice, sugar, onion, garlic, parsley sprig, *bouquet garni* seasoning and oil to the boil in a saucepan. Cover and simmer gently for 20 minutes.

4. Add the mushrooms and bring back to the boil. Simmer for a further 5 minutes, then allow the mixture to cool and chill for several hours.

5. Place the mushrooms carefully into small individual dishes and pour the marinade over them. Garnish with parsley.

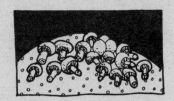

MUSHROOM COCKTAIL

Imperial (Metric)	American
6 oz (150g) button mushrooms	3 cupsful button mushrooms
¼ pint (150ml) natural yogurt	⅔ cupful natural yogurt
1 teaspoonful pure lemon juice	1 teaspoonful pure lemon juice
½ tablespoonful olive oil	½ tablespoonful olive oil
1 tablespoonful chopped chives	1 tablespoonful chopped chives
1 tablespoonful chopped parsley	1 tablespoonful chopped parsley
Seasoning to taste	Seasoning to taste
1 lettuce	1 lettuce
Paprika	Paprika

1. Wash, dry and slice the mushrooms.

2. Mix the yogurt, lemon juice, oil and herbs and add the seasoning.

3. Shred the lettuce finely and put it into four glasses.

4. Blend the mushrooms with the dressing and spoon them on top of the lettuce, then garnish with paprika.

POTATO SALAD

Imperial (Metric)	American
1½ lb (¾ kilo) new potatoes	1½ lb new potatoes
Sprig of mint	Sprig of mint
2 spring onions	2 scallions
3 tablespoonsful olive oil	3½ tablespoonsful olive oil
1 tablespoonful cider vinegar	1 tablespoonful cider vinegar
Seasoning to taste	Seasoning to taste
4 tablespoonsful chopped chives	5 tablespoonsful chopped chives

1. Wash the potatoes and cook them in their skins in boiling salted water to which the sprig of mint has been added. Drain and allow them to cool slightly, then peel and slice them thickly. Put them into a bowl.

2. Wash and chop the spring onions and add them to the potatoes.

3. Mix the oil, vinegar, seasoning and chives (reserving a few of the latter for garnishing), and pour the dressing over the potatoes and onions. Mix it in gently and garnish with the remaining chives.

RED CABBAGE SALAD

Imperial (Metric)	American
½ medium-sized red cabbage	½ medium-sized red cabbage
2 apples	2 apples
4 tablespoonful olive oil	5 tablespoonful olive oil
2 tablespoonful cider vinegar	2½ tablespoonful cider vinegar
1 teaspoonful lemon juice	1 teaspoonful lemon juice
4 teaspoonsful raw cane sugar	4 teaspoonsful raw cane sugar
Seasoning to taste	Seasoning to taste

1. Wash and shred the cabbage on a coarse grater.

2. Grate the apples, including peel.

3. Mix together the cabbage, apple, oil, vinegar, lemon juice and sugar thoroughly. Season and allow the salad to chill for about half an hour before serving.

RED CABBAGE AND BEETROOT SALAD

Imperial (Metric)
6 oz (150g) red cabbage
4 oz (100g) cooked beetroot
1 orange
2 tablespoonsful sunflower oil
2 tablespoonsful red wine vinegar
2 teaspoonsful raw cane sugar
2 oz (50g) seedless raisins

American
6 oz red cabbage
4 oz cooked beetroot
1 orange
2½ tablespoonsful sunflower oil
2½ tablespoonsful red wine vinegar
2 teaspoonsful raw cane sugar
⅓ cupful seedless raisins

1. Wash and shred the cabbage finely.

2. Dice the beetroot.

3. Peel the orange, then dice the flesh and cut the rind into matchstick shapes.

4. Combine the oil, vinegar and sugar and mix them well with the raisins.

5. Put the cabbage, beetroot and orange into a bowl and pour the dressing over them. Mix the ingredients thoroughly but gently and garnish with the strips of orange peel.

SIMPLE FRENCH BEAN SALAD

Imperial (Metric)	American
1 lb (½ kilo) French beans	1 lb snap beans
1 small onion	1 small onion
3 tablespoonsful olive oil	3½ tablespoonsful olive oil
1 tablespoonful white wine vinegar	1 tablespoonful white wine vinegar
Seasoning to taste	Seasoning to taste
½ teaspoonful dried dill	½ teaspoonful dried dill
Chopped fresh parsley	Chopped fresh parsley

1. Wash the beans and cut them into 1-in. lengths. Boil them in salted water until just tender, then drain and leave them to cool and chop the onion.

2. Combine the oil, vinegar, seasoning and dill in a jar and shake them thoroughly.

3. Put the cooled beans and chopped onion into a serving bowl and pour the dressing over, mixing it in gently. Garnish with fresh parsley and chill well before serving.

SIMPLE COURGETTE SALAD

Imperial (Metric)
1 lb (½ kilo) courgettes
Chopped parsley
Chopped basil
Chopped chives

American
1 lb zucchini
Chopped parsley
Chopped basil
Chopped chives

Dressing:

Imperial (Metric)
1 tablespoonful cider vinegar
2 tablespoonsful sunflower oil
Seasoning to taste

American
1 tablespoonful cider vinegar
2½ tablespoonsful sunflower oil
Seasoning to taste

1. Wash and pat the courgettes dry, then grate them coarsely.

2. Put the courgettes into a bowl and add the parsley, basil and chives.

3. Mix together the vinegar, oil and seasoning and pour the dressing over the salad.

SPECIAL BEETROOT SALAD

Imperial (Metric)	American
2 lb (1 kilo) cooked beetroot	2 lb cooked beet
1 large onion	1 large onion
¼ pint (150ml) white wine vinegar	⅔ cupful white wine vinegar
¼ pint (150ml) water	⅔ cupful water
1 dessertspoonful raw cane sugar	1 tablespoonful raw cane sugar
1 bay leaf	1 bay leaf
4 peppercorns	4 peppercorns
2 whole cloves	2 whole cloves
½ teaspoonful sea salt	½ teaspoonful sea salt
½ teaspoonful caraway seeds	½ teaspoonful caraway seeds

1. Cut the beetroot into slices and cut the onion into rings and place them in a deep bowl.

2. Put the vinegar in a saucepan with the water, sugar, bay leaf, peppercorns, cloves, salt, caraway seeds and peppercorns. Bring the mixture to the boil and pour it over the beetroot and onion.

3. Allow the salad to cool and then chill it well before serving.

SPICY SHALLOTS

Imperial (Metric)	American
1½ lb (¾ kilo) small shallots or button onions	1½ lb small shallots or button onions
1 large green pepper	1 large green pepper
12 black olives	12 black olives
1 oz (25g) butter	2½ tablespoonsful butter
1 small tin of tomatoes	1 small can tomatoes
1 tablespoonful cider vinegar	1 tablespoonful cider vinegar
1 tablespoonful ground cumin	1 tablespoonful ground cumin
Sea salt and freshly ground black pepper	Sea salt and freshly ground black pepper
Chopped parsley to garnish	Chopped parsley to garnish

1. Skin the shallots. De-seed and dice the pepper. Halve and stone the olives.

2. Melt the butter in a saucepan and fry the cumin for 2 minutes. Add the onions and peppers. *Sauté* gently for a few minutes, stirring well.

3. Add the tinned tomatoes, olives and vinegar. Simmer gently for about 10 minutes until the onions are cooked.

4. Season well with the cumin, salt and pepper and then pour into individual dishes. Chill well. Garnish with parsley before serving.

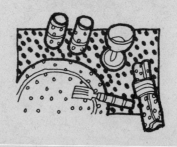

SPINACH MAYONNAISE

Imperial (Metric)	American
½ lb (¼ kilo) fresh spinach	½ lb fresh spinach
4 tablespoonsful mayonnaise	5 tablespoonsful mayonnaise
(page 14)	(page 14)
4 teaspoonsful lemon juice	4 teaspoonsful lemon juice
1 teaspoonful sea salt	1 teaspoonful sea salt
1 teaspoonful raw cane sugar	1 teaspoonful raw cane sugar

1. Wash the spinach and dry it well in a salad shaker or on a tea-towel. Chop the leaves finely, discarding the stems and damaged leaves.

2. Put the spinach into a serving bowl and mix it with the mayonnaise, lemon juice, salt and sugar.

TOMATO SALAD

Imperial (Metric)
1 lb (½ kilo) firm, ripe tomatoes
3-4 spring onions or
   1 medium-sized shallot
3 tablespoonsful sunflower oil
1 tablespoonful cider vinegar
½ teaspoonful raw cane sugar
½ teaspoonful dried dill
½ teaspoonful ready-made English
   mustard
Seasoning to taste

American
1 lb firm, ripe tomatoes
3-4 scallions or
   1 medium-sized shallot
3½ tablespoonsful sunflower oil
1 tablespoonful cider vinegar
½ teaspoonful raw cane sugar
½ teaspoonful dried dill
½ teaspoonful ready-made English
   mustard
Seasoning to taste

1. Slice the tomatoes to ¼ in. thickness and lay them in neat rows on a shallow dish.

2. Chop the onions finely.

3. In a small bowl, combine the oil, vinegar, sugar, dill, mustard and seasoning and beat them with either a fork or a wire whisk until thoroughly combined.

4. Pour the dressing over the tomatoes and garnish the salad with the chopped onions. Serve chilled.

WATERCRESS SALAD

Imperial (Metric)	American
2 bunches of watercress	2 bunches of watercress
½ cucumber	½ cucumber
8 tablespoonsful sunflower oil	10 tablespoonsful sunflower oil
3 tablespoonsful pure lemon juice	3½ tablespoonsful pure lemon juice
Seasoning to taste	Seasoning to taste
4 oz (100g) blue cheese	4 oz blue cheese

1. Wash, trim and dry the watercress, then peel and slice the cucumber and put them both into a salad bowl.

2. Mix the oil, lemon juice and seasoning in a jam jar and shake them thoroughly.

3. Pour the dressing over the salad and toss it well.

4. Crumble the blue cheese over the salad and serve immediately.

2.

RICE AND PASTA SALADS

AVOCADO RICE SALAD

Imperial (Metric)	American
½ lb (¼ kilo) brown rice	1 cupful brown rice
2 avocados	2 avocados
2 oz (50g) mushrooms	1 cupful mushrooms
3 medium-sized tomatoes	3 medium-sized tomatoes
3 spring onions	3 scallions
2 hard-boiled eggs	2 hard-boiled eggs
Approx. ¼ pint (150ml) French dressing (page 13)	Approx. ⅔ cupful French dressing (page 13)

1. Cook the rice until tender, then drain it and leave to cool.

2. Peel and stone the avocados, then cut them into cubes.

3. Wash and chop the mushrooms, tomatoes and spring onions, then peel and chop the eggs.

4. Put the rice into a deep salad bowl, add the avocado, mushrooms, eggs, tomatoes and onions and mix them gently.

5. Pour the dressing over the ingredients and mix it in thoroughly. Chill well.

CURRIED BANANA AND RICE SALAD

Imperial (Metric)	American
1 small onion	1 small onion
2 oz (50g) green pepper	2 oz green pepper
2 bananas	2 bananas
4 tablespoonsful cooked brown rice	5 tablespoonsful cooked brown rice
2 tablespoonsful unsweetened desiccated coconut	2½ tablespoonsful unsweetened desiccated coconut
2 teaspoonsful raw cane sugar	2 teaspoonsful raw cane sugar
½ teaspoonful sea salt	½ teaspoonful sea salt
2 tablespoonsful lemon juice	2½ tablespoonsful lemon juice
4 tablespoonsful sunflower oil	5 tablespoonsful sunflower oil
Chopped fresh parsley	Chopped fresh parsley

1. Peel and chop the onion, de-seed and slice the pepper thinly then peel and dice the bananas.

2. Place the onion, pepper and bananas in a deep serving bowl with the brown rice and coconut.

3. Place the sugar, sea salt, curry powder, lemon juice and oil in a jam jar and shake it well.

4. Pour the dressing over the salad, mix it in carefully and garnish the salad with the parsley. Chill before serving.

← 2 large bananas

CURRIED PASTA SALAD

Imperial (Metric)	American
4 oz (100g) wholewheat pasta shells	2 cupsful wholewheat pasta shells
4 oz (100g) mushrooms	2 cupsful mushrooms
1 dessertspoonful polyunsaturated margarine or butter	1 tablespoonful polyunsaturated margarine or butter
1 large onion	1 large onion
2 tablespoonsful dry Vermouth	2½ tablespoonsful dry Vermouth
5 tablespoonsful mayonnaise (page 14)	6 tablespoonsful mayonnaise (page 14)
1 teaspoonful curry paste	1 teaspoonful curry paste
1 teaspoonful raw sugar apricot jam	1 teaspoonful raw sugar apricot jam
Seasoning to taste	Seasoning to taste
Finely sliced rings of green pepper	Finely sliced rings of green pepper

1. Cook the pasta in boiling salted water, then drain it and allow to cool.

2. Wash and slice the mushrooms and *sauté* them in the margarine or butter until tender.

3. Chop the onion and put it in a saucepan. Add the Vermouth, bring to the boil and simmer for 3 minutes and allow to cool.

4. Put the onion mixture, mayonnaise, curry paste, apricot jam and lemon juice into a bowl and mix them well. Season to taste, add the pasta and mushrooms and mix them in gently. Chill the salad well and, before serving, arrange it on a shallow dish and garnish with sliced green pepper.

FRUITY RICE SALAD

Imperial (Metric)
½ lb (¼ kilo) brown rice
4 large bananas
1 red eating apple
2 tablespoonful walnuts
3 oz (75g) pineapple
4 oz (100g) grapes
1 tablespoonful sultanas
4 large lettuce leaves
Unsweetened desiccated coconut

American
1 cupful brown rice
4 large bananas
1 red eating apple
2½ tablespoonsful English walnuts
3 oz pineapple
4 oz grapes
1 tablespoonful golden seedless
   raisins
4 large lettuce leaves
Unsweetened desiccated coconut

Dressing:

Imperial (Metric)
½ pint (¼ litre) mayonnaise
   (page 14)
2 tablespoonsful lemon juice
Pinch of chilli powder

American
1⅓ cupful mayonnaise
   (page 14)
2½ tablespoonsful lemon juice
Pinch of chilli powder

1. Cook the rice until tender, then drain it and allow to cool.

2. Peel the bananas and slice them finely, core and chop the apple, then chop the walnuts and pineapple.

3. Put the cooled rice into a bowl and mix in the bananas, apple, grapes, pineapple, walnuts and sultanas.

4. In another bowl mix the mayonnaise, lemon juice and chilli powder and stir it into the rice mixture.

5. Arrange the lettuce leaves around the outside of a serving bowl and place the rice mixture in the centre. Garnish the salad with the coconut.

GREEN RICE

Imperial (Metric)	American
4 oz (100g) brown rice	½ cupful brown rice
3 tablespoonsful olive oil	3½ tablespoonsful olive oil
2 teaspoonsful cider vinegar	2 teaspoonsful cider vinegar
Squeeze of lemon juice	Squeeze of lemon juice
Seasoning to taste	Seasoning to taste
2 tablespoonsful chopped parsley	2½ tablespoonsful chopped parsley
2 tablespoonsful chopped chives	2½ tablespoonsful chopped chives
1 tablespoonful chopped dill	1 tablespoonful chopped dill
1 tablespoonful chopped tarragon	1 tablespoonful chopped tarragon

1. Cook the rice, drain it well and, while still warm, stir in the oil, vinegar, lemon juice and seasoning.

2. When cool, stir in the chopped herbs. Chill the rice before serving.

MACARONI SALAD

Imperial (Metric)	American
4 oz (100g) wholewheat macaroni	1 cupful wholewheat macaroni
3 tablespoonsful French dressing (page 13)	3½ tablespoonsful French dressing (page 13)
2 oz (50g) almond flakes	½ cupful almond flakes
½ teaspoonful paprika	½ teaspoonful paprika
2 oz (50g) button mushrooms, washed	1 cupful button mushrooms, washed
1 tablespoonful chopped chives	1 tablespoonful chopped chives
1 tangerine or mandarin orange	1 tangerine or mandarin orange

1. Cook the macaroni in boiling salted water, drain it thoroughly, rinse and allow to cool.

2. Put the macaroni in a large bowl and add the French dressing, almonds, paprika, mushrooms and chives.

3. Peel and de-pith the tangerine or mandarin orange and divide it into segments. Add this to the rest of the salad and toss it thoroughly.

MOROCCAN RICE SALAD

Imperial (Metric)	American
6 oz (150g) brown rice	¾ cupful brown rice
2 bananas	2 bananas
1 small cucumber	1 small cucumber
2 tablespoonsful seedless raisins	2½ tablespoonsful seedless raisins
1 tablespoonful chopped almonds	1 tablespoonful chopped almonds
4 tablespoonsful olive oil	5 tablespoonsful olive oil
4 tablespoonsful lemon juice	5 tablespoonsful lemon juice
Grated rind of ½ lemon	Grated rind of ½ lemon
½ teaspoonful ground coriander	½ teaspoonful ground coriander
½ teaspoonful ground cumin	½ teaspoonful ground cumin
½ teaspoonful cayenne pepper	½ teaspoonful cayenne pepper
1 teaspoonful clear honey	1 teaspoonful clear honey
1 teaspoonful sea salt	1 teaspoonful sea salt

1. Cook the rice, then drain it and allow to cool.

2. Peel and slice the bananas and slice the cucumber.

3. Put the rice into a deep salad bowl. Add the cucumber, raisins, almonds and bananas and mix them in gently.

4. Put the oil, lemon juice and rind, coriander, cumin, cayenne pepper, honey and sea salt into a jam jar and shake the mixture well. Pour the dressing over the rice and chill before serving.

PASTA AND BEANSPROUT SALAD

Imperial (Metric)	American
4 oz (100g) wholewheat noodles	1 cupful wholewheat noodles
7 tablespoonsful sunflower oil	½ cupful sunflower oil
1 bunch of watercress	1 bunch of watercress
3 cupsful beansprouts	3¾ cupsful beansprouts
2 tomatoes	2 tomatoes
3 oz (75g) cashew nuts, chopped and toasted	⅔ cupful cashew nuts, chopped and toasted
1 oz (25g) wheatgerm, toasted	¼ cupful wheatgerm toasted
1 oz (25g) sesame seeds, toasted	2½ tablespoonsful sesame seeds, toasted
6 tablespoonsful lemon juice	½ cupful lemon juice
Seasoning to taste	Seasoning to taste

1. Cook the noodles until tender. Drain them well, place them in a bowl and mix in 1 tablespoonful of the sunflower oil. Set aside to chill.

2. Wash, trim and drain the watercress, the beansprouts, and chop the tomatoes finely.

3. Arrange the noodles around the outside of a large serving platter, followed by a ring of watercress, then a ring of beansprouts, finishing off with a ring of tomatoes and chopped nuts in the centre.

4. Mix the wheatgerm, sesame seeds, lemon juice, oil and seasoning together and pour the dressing over the salad.

PASTA SHELLS AND BEANSPROUT SALAD

Imperial (Metric)	American
½ lb (¼ kilo) wholewheat pasta shells	4 cupsful wholewheat pasta shells
2 spring onions	2 scallions
½ red pepper	½ red pepper
2 sticks of celery	2 sticks of celery
1 tablespoonful soy sauce	1 tablespoonful soy sauce
5 oz (125g) beansprouts	2½ cupsful beansprouts
2 oz (50g) cashew nuts	½ cupful cashew nuts
2 tablespoonsful sunflower oil	2½ tablespoonsful sunflower oil
Seasoning to taste	Seasoning to taste

1. Cook the pasta shells then drain them and set them aside to chill.

2. Chop the onions, red pepper and celery.

3. Put the pasta shells in a bowl and stir in the soy sauce, onions, pepper, celery, beansprouts and cashew nuts with the oil. Season well.

RICE AND ORANGE SALAD

Imperial (Metric)	American
½ lb (¼ kilo) cooked brown rice	1⅓ cupful cooked brown rice
2 oranges	2 oranges
1 clove garlic	1 clove garlic
1 dessertspoonful pure orange juice	1 tablespoonful pure orange juice
2 heads of chicory	2 heads of chicory
3 oz (75g) walnut pieces	⅔ cupful walnut pieces
3 oz (75g) raisins	½ cupful raisins
1 tablespoonful sunflower oil	1 tablespoonful sunflower oil
Seasoning to taste	Seasoning to taste
Grated rind of ½ orange	Grated rind of ½ orange

1. Put the rice into a large, deep bowl.

2. Peel and cut the oranges into segments and cut each segment in half. Crush the garlic and add it to the orange juice.

3. Cut one head of chicory into thin slices. Mix the chicory, orange, orange juice, walnuts, raisins and sunflower oil thoroughly with the rice and season well.

4. Slice the second chicory head and arrange it around the outside of the bowl with the rice mixture piled in the middle.

5. Garnish with the grated orange rind.

RICE RING

Imperial (Metric)	American
½ lb (¼ kilo) long-grain brown rice	1 cupful long-grain brown rice
2 large tomatoes	2 large tomatoes
1 red pepper	1 red pepper
4 teaspoonsful chopped fresh chives	4 teaspoonsful chopped fresh chives
4 teaspoonsful chopped fresh parsley	4 teaspoonsful chopped fresh parsley
½ teaspoonful dried oregano	½ teaspoonful dried oregano
½ teaspoonful dried basil	½ teaspoonful dried basil
10 green olives	10 green olives
4 tablespoonsful olive oil	5 tablespoonsful olive oil
2 tablespoonsful cider vinegar	2½ tablespoonsful cider vinegar
1 teaspoonful lemon juice	1 teaspoonful lemon juice
Seasoning to taste	Seasoning to taste
Black olives and watercress	Black olives and watercress

1. Cook rice in boiling salted water until tender. Drain.

2. Skin and chop the tomatoes. Blanch the pepper in boiling water for 5 minutes. De-seed and cut into narrow strips.

3. Put the warmed rice in a large bowl and add the tomatoes, chives, parsley, oregano, basil and the pepper. Chop and add the green olives.

4. Mix the oil, vinegar, lemon juice and seasoning and pour enough dressing over the rice mixture to moisten the salad well.

5. Press the mixture firmly into a small ring mould that has been previously oiled and chill the rice well.

6. Turn out the ring on to a serving dish and garnish with black olives and watercress.

SALAD CREOLE

Imperial (Metric)	**American**
2 tomatoes	2 tomatoes
½ red pepper	½ red pepper
1 medium-sized onion	1 medium-sized onion
3 oz (75g) cooked brown rice	½ cupful cooked brown rice
3 tablespoonsful cooked peas	3½ tablespoonsful cooked peas
2 teaspoonsful chopped fresh parsley	2 teaspoonsful chopped fresh parsley
1 teaspoonful raw cane sugar	1 teaspoonful raw cane sugar
1 tablespoonful cider vinegar	1 tablespoonful cider vinegar
3 tablespoonsful mayonnaise (page 14)	3½ tablespoonsful mayonnaise (page 14)
Seasoning to taste	Seasoning to taste

1. Cut the tomatoes into small cubes.

2. Chop the pepper and onion finely.

3. Mix together the rice, onion, peas, tomatoes, pepper and parsley.

4. Make a dressing from the sugar, vinegar, mayonnaise and seasoning.

5. Mix the salad ingredients and dressing in a bowl and chill well.

SPAGHETTI SALAD

Imperial (Metric)	American
4 oz (100g) wholewheat spaghetti	½ cupful wholewheat spaghetti
1 carrot, cooked	1 carrot, cooked
1 tomato	1 tomato
2 spring onions, chopped	2 scallions, chopped
2 gherkins, chopped	2 gherkins, chopped
1 tablespoonful chopped fresh parsley	1 tablespoonful chopped fresh parsley
1 teaspoonful raw cane sugar	1 teaspoonful raw cane sugar
1 teaspoonful sea salt	1 teaspoonful sea salt
4 tablespoonsful mayonnaise (page 14)	5 tablespoonsful mayonnaise (page 14)

1. Cook the spaghetti and cut it into 2-in. lengths.

2. Dice the carrot and tomato.

3. Put all the ingredients into a bowl and mix them gently, then chill the salad for about half an hour before serving.

SPANISH RICE SALAD

Imperial (Metric)	American
4 oz (100g) long-grain brown rice	½ cupful long-grain brown rice
2 spring onions	2 scallions
2 cloves garlic, crushed	2 cloves garlic, crushed
½ cupful finely chopped parsley	½ cupful finely chopped parsley
6 tablespoonsful olive oil	½ cupful olive oil
1 tablespoonful cider vinegar	1 tablespoonful cider vinegar
1 teaspoonful paprika	1 teaspoonful paprika
Seasoning to taste	Seasoning to taste
1 lb (½ kilo) tomatoes	1 lb tomatoes
4 hard-boiled eggs	4 hard-boiled eggs
2 red peppers	2 red peppers
1 tablespoonful chopped fresh marjoram	1 tablespoonful chopped fresh marjoram

1. Cook the rice in boiling salted water until tender. Drain it well and allow to cool, then place it in a serving bowl.

2. Chop the spring onions and add them to the rice with the garlic, parsley, oil, vinegar, paprika and seasoning. Arrange the mixture in the centre of a large serving dish.

3. Quarter the tomatoes and eggs, slice and de-seed the peppers and arrange these around the rice mixture. Garnish with the chopped marjoram.

TUSCAN SALAD

Imperial (Metric)	American
½ lb (¼ kilo) brown rice	1 cupful brown rice
4 tablespoonsful dry white wine	5 tablespoonsful dry white wine
1 green pepper	1 green pepper
1 red pepper	1 red pepper
1 small cucumber	1 small cucumber
2 spring onions	2 scallions
12 stuffed green olives	12 stuffed green olives
4 oz (100g) cooked white haricot beans	½ cupful cooked white navy beans

Dressing:

Imperial (Metric)	American
6 tablespoonsful olive oil	½ cupful olive oil
3 tablespoonsful red wine vinegar	3½ tablespoonsful red wine vinegar
1 clove garlic, crushed	1 clove garlic, crushed
1 teaspoonful dried basil	1 teaspoonful dried basil
Seasoning to taste	Seasoning to taste

1. Cook the rice and drain it well. Stir in the white wine and leave to cool.

2. De-seed and thinly slice the peppers, peel and dice the cucumber, chop the onions and halve the olives.

3. When the rice is cold put it into a bowl and add the peppers, cucumber, onions, olives and beans and mix them well.

4. Make a dressing with the oil, vinegar, garlic and basil. Season to taste and pour the mixture over the rice mixture. Mix and chill well.

3.

MAIN COURSE SALADS

AVOCADO AND CREAM CHEESE

Imperial (Metric)	American
2 firm tomatoes	2 firm tomatoes
½ clove garlic	½ clove garlic
1 small onion	1 small onion
1 avocado pear	1 avocado pear
Seasoning to taste	Seasoning to taste
Lettuce leaves	Lettuce leaves

1. Chop one of the tomatoes, peel and crush the garlic and peel and chop onion.

2. Peel the avocado and cut it in half lengthways. Remove the stone. Cut the flesh into large pieces and mash them roughly with a fork.

3. Mash the cream cheese until smooth and gradually add the avocado. Beat the mixture thoroughly.

4. Stir in the onion, garlic and chopped tomato and season well.

5. Arrange the lettuce on four small plates, pile the avocado mixture on the lettuce and top with tomato slices. Serve with warm pitta bread.

AVOCADO AND EGG SALAD

Imperial (Metric)	American
2 ripe avocado pears	2 ripe avocado pears
2 hard-boiled eggs	2 hard-boiled eggs
2 tablespoonsful rolled oats	2½ tablespoonsful rolled oats
1 teaspoonful chopped fresh parsley	1 teaspoonful chopped fresh parsley
1 teaspoonful chopped fresh chives	1 teaspoonful chopped fresh chives
1 tomato	1 tomato
Seasoning to taste	Seasoning to taste
3 tablespoonsful mayonnaise (page 14)	3½ tablespoonsful mayonnaise (page 14)
Lettuce leaves	Lettuce leaves

1. Cut the avocados in half lengthways and remove the stones.

2. Chop the eggs finely and mix them with the oats, parsley and chives.

3. Chop the tomato into small cubes and add it to the egg mixture. Season and mix in the mayonnaise.

4. Heap the mixture on the avocado halves and serve each one on a bed of lettuce garnished with a little extra chopped parsley.

BEETROOT AND EGG SALAD

Imperial (Metric)	American
1 lb (½ kilo) cooked beetroot	1 lb cooked beet
1 onion	1 onion
4 hard-boiled eggs	4 hard-boiled eggs
Approx. ¼ pint (150ml) French dressing (page 13)	Approx. ⅔ cupful French dressing (page 13)
Chopped fresh parsley	Chopped fresh parsley

1. Peel and grate the beetroot and the onion.

2. Cut the eggs in half and remove the yolks. Rub them through a fine sieve and chop the whites into small pieces.

3. Put the beetroot, onion, eggs and dressing into a bowl and mix them gently.

4. Garnish the salad with chopped egg white and parsley.

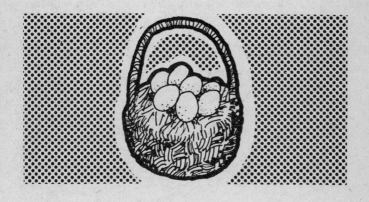

BRAZIL NUT SALAD

Imperial (Metric)	American
1 crisp lettuce	1 crisp lettuce
3 bananas	3 bananas
1 tablespoonful lemon juice	1 tablespoonful lemon juice
4 oz (100g) Brazil nuts	¾ cupful Brazil nuts
4 tablespoonsful French dressing (page 13)	5 tablespoonsful French dressing (page 13)

1. Separate the lettuce into leaves and wash and dry them thoroughly. Arrange half of the leaves around a shallow bowl and shred the rest.

2. Peel and slice the bananas thinly and sprinkle them with lemon juice. Chop the Brazil nuts.

3. Put the shredded lettuce, Brazil nuts and half the bananas in the centre of the serving bowl, pour over the French dressing and mix it in carefully.

4. Arrange the remaining slices of banana around the outside of the mixture in a ring.

CAESAR SALAD

Imperial (Metric)	American
4 slices wholemeal bread	4 slices wholemeal bread
5 tablespoonsful sunflower oil	6 tablespoonsful sunflower oil
1 clove garlic	1 clove garlic
1 large Cos lettuce	1 large Cos lettuce
1 large endive, chopped	1 large endive, chopped
1 oz (25g) grated Parmesan cheese	¼ cupful Parmesan cheese
2 oz (50g) crumbled blue cheese	½ cupful crumbled blue cheese
3 tablespoonsful lemon juice	3½ tablespoonsful lemon juice
¼ teaspoonful Tabasco sauce	½ teaspoonful Tabasco sauce
¾ teaspoonful sea salt	¾ teaspoonful sea salt
1 raw egg	1 raw egg

1. Remove the crusts from the bread and dice it.

2. Heat up 2 tablespoonsful of the oil. Chop the garlic clove and add the diced bread and garlic to the oil. *Sauté* them until lightly browned, then drain them and set to one side.

3. Tear the lettuce into bite-sized pieces and place it in a salad bowl with the endive. Sprinkle the Parmesan and blue cheese over the top.

4. Make a dressing with the remainder of the oil, lemon juice, Tabasco sauce, mustard and seasoning in a jam jar. Shake well and pour the mixture over the salad, tossing it lightly.

5. Break the egg into the salad and mix it in gently until egg particles disappear.

6. Add the *croûtons* and toss the salad lightly again.

CHICK PEA SALAD

Imperial (Metric)	American
6 oz (150g) dried chick peas	¾ cupful dried garbanzo beans
1 small onion	1 small onion
½ small clove garlic	½ small clove garlic
Juice of 1 lemon	Juice of 1 lemon
3 dessertspoonsful olive oil	3 tablespoonsful olive oil
½ teaspoonful sea salt	½ teaspoonful sea salt
Cayenne pepper	Cayenne pepper
3 tablespoonsful finely chopped parsley	3½ tablespoonsful finely chopped parsley

1. Soak the chick peas overnight in enough cold water to cover them. In the morning, drain the peas and put them in a saucepan covered with cold water. Simmer the peas for about 1½ hours, topping up with more cold water when necessary. Drain them and allow to cool.

2. Peel and chop the onion and garlic finely.

3. Mix together the lemon juice, olive oil, garlic, salt and cayenne pepper.

4. Put the peas and the chopped onion into a bowl, pour the dressing over them and mix thoroughly. Chill well before serving, garnished with parsley.

COLD RATATOUILLE SALAD

Imperial (Metric)	American
2 medium-sized onions	2 medium-sized onions
2 green peppers	2 green peppers
4 tablespoonsful olive oil	5 tablespoonsful olive oil
1 clove garlic, crushed	1 clove garlic, crushed
1 lb (½ kilo) courgettes	1 lb zucchini
2 medium-sized aubergines	2 medium-sized eggplants
1 lb (½ kilo) tomatoes	1 lb tomatoes
1 tablespoonful raw cane sugar	1 tablespoonful raw cane sugar
Seasoning to taste	Seasoning to taste
A few black olives	A few black olives
Parsley to garnish	Parsley to garnish

1. Peel and slice the onions, de-seed and chop the green peppers.

2. Heat the olive oil in a heavy pan and add the onions, peppers and garlic. Cook them for about 15 minutes, stirring occasionally.

3. Slice the courgettes, cut the aubergines into chunks and add them to the onion and pepper mixture. Cook for a further 20 minutes.

4. Skin the tomatoes, chop them coarsely and add them to the cooked mixture with the sugar. Season well and cook for a further 10 minutes. (When cooked, the vegetables should be tender and the liquid well reduced and thick.) Chill the salad well and season again before serving. Garnish with the olives and the parsley.

COURGETTE AND CHEESE SALAD

Imperial (Metric)	American
2 hard-boiled eggs	2 hard-boiled eggs
2 medium-sized courgettes	2 medium-sized zucchini
1 small onion	1 small onion
1 small lettuce	1 small lettuce
4 oz (100g) grated cheese	1 cupful grated cheese
¼ teaspoonful dried dill	½ teaspoonful dried dill

Dressing:

Imperial (Metric)	American
1 tablespoonful olive oil	1 tablespoonful olive oil
1 tablespoonful cider vinegar	1 tablespoonful cider vinegar
¼ teaspoonful raw cane sugar	¼ teaspoonful raw cane sugar
¼ teaspoonful ready-made mustard	¼ teaspoonful ready-made mustard
½ clove garlic, crushed	½ clove garlic, crushed
Seasoning to taste	Seasoning to taste

1. Chop the eggs and grate the courgettes.

2. Peel and slice the onion, then wash, dry and shred the lettuce.

3. Put the lettuce, courgettes, cheese and onion into a bowl.

4. Make a dressing with the olive oil, vinegar, sugar, mustard and garlic. Season and mix well.

5. Pour the dressing over the salad, toss it lightly and garnish with the dried dill.

CRACKED WHEAT SALAD

Imperial (Metric)	American
6 oz (150g) cracked wheat	1 cupful cracked wheat
1 bunch of spring onions	1 bunch of scallions
½ lb (¼ kilo) tomatoes	½ lb tomatoes
½ cupful chopped fresh parsley	½ cupful chopped fresh parsley
¼ pint (150ml) sunflower oil	⅔ cupful sunflower oil
2 tablespoonsful lemon juice	2½ tablespoonsful lemon juice
Seasoning to taste	Seasoning to taste

1. Soak the cracked wheat in cold water for about 45 minutes, then drain it and squeeze out as much water as possible.

2. Chop up the spring onions and tomatoes.

3. Put the wheat into a bowl and mix it with the onions, tomatoes and parsley.

4. Make a dressing with the oil and lemon juice, add seasoning and mix it into the salad.

GOUDA IN CUCUMBER SHELLS

Imperial (Metric)	American
2 medium-sized cucumbers	2 medium-sized cucumbers
1 red-skinned apple	1 red-skinned apple
4 oz (100g) mushrooms	2 cupsful mushrooms
1 onion	1 onion
4 oz (100g) finely grated Gouda cheese	1 cupful finely grated Gouda cheese
1 teaspoonful ready-made French mustard	1 teaspoonful ready-made French mustard
4 tablespoonsful mayonnaise (page 14)	5 tablespoonsful mayonnaise (page 14)
Seasoning to taste	Seasoning to taste
8 stuffed olives, sliced	8 stuffed olives, sliced
Parsley sprigs	Parsley sprigs

1. Halve the cucumbers and scoop out the seeds, then cut each piece into four.

2. Plunge the cucumbers into boiling water for about 1 minute, then drain them and leave them to cool.

3. Core and chop the apple then chop the mushrooms. Peel and chop the onion.

4. Put all the ingredients except the cucumber in a bowl. Season and mix them well.

5. Pile the mixture into the cucumber shells and decorate with the sliced olives and parsley sprigs.

GREEK SUMMER SALAD

Imperial (Metric)	American
1 lettuce	1 lettuce
12 spring onions	12 scallions
6 large, firm tomatoes	6 large, firm tomatoes
½ cucumber, scored with a fork	½ cucumber, scored with a fork
12 sprigs of fresh mint, chopped	12 sprigs of fresh mint, chopped
1 teaspoonful dried marjoram or oregano	1 teaspoonful dried marjoram or oregano
4 tablespoonsful olive oil	5 tablespoonsful olive oil
2 tablespoonsful lemon juice	2½ tablespoonsful lemon juice
Seasoning to taste	Seasoning to taste
6 oz (150g) féta cheese	¾ cupful féta cheese
18 black olives	18 black olives

1. Wash the lettuce, then drain it and divide it into leaves. Roll up each leaf and slice it finely.

2. Scatter the lettuce on a large serving dish.

3. Chop the spring onions, then slice tomatoes and cucumber and arrange them on the lettuce. Garnish with the onions and herbs.

4. Beat together the oil, lemon juice and seasoning and pour the dressing over salad.

5. Crumble the cheese over the top of the salad and garnish with black olives.

INDIVIDUAL CREAM CHEESE
AND WATERCRESS SALADS

Imperial (Metric)	American
1 bunch of watercress	1 bunch of watercress
1 lb (½ kilo) tomatoes	1 lb tomatoes
6 oz (150g) cream cheese	¾ cupful cream cheese
4 tablespoonsful chopped chives	5 tablespoonsful chopped chives
Seasoning to taste	Seasoning to taste
3 tablespoonsful olive oil	3½ tablespoonsful olive oil
½ teaspoonful raw cane sugar	½ teaspoonful raw cane sugar
½ teaspoonful mustard	½ teaspoonful mustard
1 tablespoonful cider vinegar	1 tablespoonful cider vinegar

1. Wash and dry the watercress then pick out a few sprigs and decorate the rims of four small dishes.

2. Slice the tomatoes and arrange them in the centre of each dish.

3. Form the cream cheese into four balls and roll them in the chopped chives. Pat this mixture on top of the tomatoes. Season and chill well.

4. Mix together the oil, sugar, mustard and vinegar and pour this dressing over the individual salads just before serving.

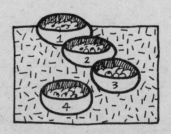

ITALIAN SALAD

Imperial (Metric)	American
1 lb (½ kilo) any cooked root vegetable (carrots, parsnips, turnips, swedes)	1 lb any cooked root vegetable (carrots, parsnips, turnips, rutabagas)
1 large apple	1 large apple
1 leek	1 leek
3 gherkins	3 gherkins
2 tablespoonsful cooked peas	2½ tablespoonsful cooked peas
2 tablespoonsful cooked white haricot beans	2½ tablespoonsful cooked white navy beans
4 tablespoonsful mayonnaise (page 14)	5 tablespoonsful mayonnaise (page 14)
2 tablespoonsful cider vinegar	2½ tablespoonsful cider vinegar
1 teaspoonful chopped fresh parsley	1 teaspoonful chopped fresh parsley
1 teaspoonful chopped chives	1 teaspoonful chopped chives
Seasoning to taste	Seasoning to taste

1. Dice the cooked root vegetable of your choice and the apple.

2. Slice the leek finely. Chop up the gherkins and mix all the vegetables and apple together in a serving dish.

3. Mix the mayonnaise with the vinegar, herbs and seasoning and carefully combine the dressing with the vegetables. Chill and serve.

ITALIAN SUMMER SALAD

Imperial (Metric)	American
3 tomatoes	3 tomatoes
½ cucumber	½ cucumber
4 cooked artichoke hearts	4 cooked artichoke hearts
½ lb (¼ kilo) cooked French beans	1 cupful cooked snap beans
1 lb (½ kilo) cooked asparagus spears (tinned or fresh)	1 lb cooked asparagus spears (tinned or fresh)
A few black olives	A few black olives

Dressing:

Imperial (Metric)	American
¼ pint (150ml) olive oil	⅔ cupful olive oil
3 tablespoonsful white wine vinegar	3½ tablespoonsful white wine vinegar
1 teaspoonful basil	1 teaspoonful basil
Seasoning to taste	Seasoning to taste

1. Roughly chop the tomatoes and peel and slice the cucumber finely.

2. Put all the vegetables except the olives into a salad bowl.

3. Mix the oil, vinegar, basil and seasoning in a jam jar and shake it thoroughly.

4. Pour the dressing over the salad and toss it thoroughly but gently. Chill for about an hour.

5. Garnish with the olives before serving.

LEEK AND EGG WITH YOGURT

Imperial (Metric)	American
12 small leeks	12 small leeks
2 spring onions, chopped	2 scallions, chopped
2 hard-boiled eggs	2 hard-boiled eggs

Dressing:

Imperial (Metric)	American
½ clove garlic	½ clove garlic
¼ pint (150ml) olive oil	⅔ cupful olive oil
1 teaspoonful ready-made French mustard	1 teaspoonful ready-made French mustard
1 tablespoonful white wine vinegar	1 tablespoonful white wine vinegar
3 tablespoonsful natural yogurt	3½ tablespoonsful natural yogurt
Seasoning to taste	Seasoning to taste

1. Cook the leeks in salted water and leave them to cool.

2. Crush the garlic and mix together the oil, mustard and vinegar. Add the garlic and shake the mixture well in a jam jar. Stir in the yogurt and seasoning.

3. Chop the spring onions and hard-boiled eggs finely.

4. Lay the leeks on a dish and cover them with the chopped egg. Pour the dressing over and then garnish with the chopped onions.

LENTIL SALAD

Imperial (Metric)	American
½ lb (¼ kilo) brown lentils	1 cupful brown lentils
4 tablespoonsful French dressing (page 13)	5 tablespoonsful French dressing (page 13)
1 small red pepper	1 small red pepper
1 onion	1 onion
2 sticks of celery	2 sticks of celery
Sea salt and freshly ground black pepper	Sea salt and freshly ground black pepper
Chopped parsley	Chopped parsley

1. Cover the lentils with boiling water and leave them to soak for half an hour. Drain, cover with fresh water, bring to the boil and cook gently until tender (about 40 minutes). Drain well and mix with the French dressing while still warm.

2. Core, de-seed and chop the pepper. Peel and slice the onion and chop the celery. Add all these ingredients to the lentil mixture. Season well and chill.

3. Garnish with chopped parsley before serving.

NEW POTATO SALAD WITH CURRY DRESSING

Imperial (Metric)	American
1½ lb (¾ kilo) new potatoes	1½ lb new potatoes
1 clove garlic, crushed	1 clove garlic, crushed
1 tablespoonful cider vinegar	1 tablespoonful cider vinegar
Seasoning to taste	Seasoning to taste
1 green pepper	1 green pepper
¼ pint (150ml) double cream	⅔ cupful heavy cream
2 tablespoonsful mayonnaise (page 14)	2½ tablespoonsful mayonnaise (page 14)
Juice of ½ lemon	Juice of ½ lemon
1 teaspoonful curry powder	1 teaspoonful curry powder
Chopped parsley	Chopped parsley

1. Wash and scrub the potatoes well and boil them until tender (about 15 minutes).

2. When the potatoes have cooled slightly, peel and slice them thickly.

3. Rub the garlic round the salad bowl and add the potatoes.

4. While the potatoes are still warm, pour the vinegar over them and season well.

5. Chop and de-seed the green pepper and mix it with the potatoes.

6. Combine the cream, mayonnaise, lemon juice and curry powder, pour the dressing over the potatoes and mix it in gently. Chill well before serving with chopped parsley.

NUTTY MUSHROOM SALAD

Imperial (Metric)	American
6 oz (150g) mushrooms	3 cupful mushrooms
2 oz (50g) walnut pieces	½ cupful English walnut pieces
½ teaspoonful sea salt	½ teaspoonful sea salt
3 tablespoonsful sunflower oil	3½ tablespoonsful sunflower oil
2 tablespoonsful lemon juice	2½ tablespoonsful lemon juice
1 teaspoonful honey	1 teaspoonful honey
1 teaspoonful chopped fresh ginger	1 teaspoonful chopped fresh ginger
or ½ teaspoonful ground ginger	or ½ teaspoonful ground ginger
Small bunch of washed watercress	Small bunch of washed watercress

1. Wash, dry and thinly slice the mushrooms, then place them in a salad bowl with the walnuts.

2. Shake the salt, oil, lemon juice, honey and ginger together in a jam jar until thoroughly blended.

3. Pour the dressing over the mushrooms and walnuts and pile the mixture into the centre of the bowl.

4. Garnish the edges with watercress.

OMELETTE SALAD

Imperial (Metric)
Olive oil for frying
2 eggs
1 tablespoonful milk
Sea salt and freshly ground
  black pepper to taste
1 dessert apple
1 red pepper
4 oz (100g) mushrooms
2 large cooked potatoes
1 lettuce
12 green stuffed olives, sliced
French dressing (page 13) to which
  1 tablespoonful dry sherry has
  been added
1 oz (25g) almond flakes

American
Olive oil for frying
2 eggs
1 tablespoonful milk
Sea salt and freshly ground
  black pepper to taste
1 dessert apple
1 red pepper
2 cupsful mushrooms
2 large cooked potatoes
1 lettuce
12 green stuffed olives, stuffed
French dressing (page 13) to which
  1 tablespoonful dry sherry has
  been added
¼ cupful almond flakes

1. Make the omelette by heating the oil in an omelette pan; mix the eggs, milk, salt and pepper and pour into pan. Fry gently until the mixture is set.

2. Turn the omelette out and allow to cool. Then cut into small squares.

3. Core and slice the apple, then de-seed the pepper and cut into strips. Wash and slice the mushrooms thinly, dice the potatoes and wash and separate the lettuce. Dry thoroughly.

4. Arrange the lettuce leaves around a serving bowl and place the mushrooms, peppers, potatoes, olives, apple and omelette on top. Pour over the French dressing and sprinkle with flaked almonds.

PINE NUT SALAD

Imperial (Metric)	American
1 cucumber	1 cucumber
1 green apple	1 green apple
1 bunch of watercress	1 bunch of watercress
1 bunch of radishes	1 bunch of radishes
1 crisp lettuce heart	1 crisp lettuce heart
2 oz (50g) pine nuts	3½ tablespoonsful pine nuts
3 tablespoonsful sunflower oil	3½ tablespoonsful sunflower oil
Juice of 1 lemon	Juice of 1 lemon
Seasoning to taste	Seasoning to taste

1. Peel and dice the cucumber, then chop the apple, watercress, radishes and lettuce.

2. Mix the cucumber, radishes, watercress, pine nuts and apple in a bowl.

3. Make a dressing with the oil, lemon juice and seasoning.

4. Pour the dressing over the salad and mix it in gently.

dice the cucumber
chop the apple

PRUNE, WALNUT AND COTTAGE CHEESE SALAD

Imperial (Metric)
1 large lettuce
½ lb (¼ kilo) plain cottage cheese
3 oz (75g) chopped walnuts
½ lb (¼ kilo) prunes, soaked and
   stoned
Vinaigrette dressing (optional)
   (page 13)

American
1 large lettuce
1 cupful plain cottage cheese
⅔ cupful chopped English walnuts
1½ cupsful prunes, soaked and
   stoned
Vinaigrette dressing (optional)
   (page 13)

1. Arrange the lettuce on a serving dish.

2. Pile the cottage cheese in the centre and garnish with the walnuts.

3. Chop the prunes and sprinkle them around the edge of the dish. If used, serve the dressing separately.

SALAD ROULADE

Imperial (Metric)	American
½ Webbs lettuce	½ Webbs lettuce
2 tomatoes	2 tomatoes
1 oz (25g) mushrooms	½ cupful mushrooms
2 small spring onions	2 small scallions
A little Parmesan cheese, grated	A little Parmesan cheese, grated
6 oz (150g) grated cheese	1½ cupsful grated cheese
2 oz (50g) fresh wholemeal breadcrumbs	1 cupful fresh wholemeal breadcrumbs
4 eggs	4 eggs
¼ pint (150ml) single cream	⅔ cupful single cream
Seasoning to taste	Seasoning to taste
1 teaspoonful ready-made mustard	1 teaspoonful ready-made mustard
2 tablespoonsful warm water	2½ tablespoonsful warm water
4 tablespoonsful mayonnaise (page 14)	5 tablespoonsful mayonnaise (page 14)
Parsley to garnish	Parsley to garnish

1. Heat the oven to 400°F/200°C (Gas Mark 6).

2. Wash and dry the lettuce and shred it finely, then wash and slice the tomatoes and mushrooms thinly. Chop the spring onions.

3. Line a Swiss roll tin (approximately 13×9 in./33×23cm) with greaseproof paper and sprinkle with the grated Parmesan.

4. Mix the grated cheese and breadcrumbs together in a bowl.

5. Separate the eggs and add the yolks to the cheese and bread-crumb mixture. Also add the cream, seasoning and mustard and stir in the warm water to make a fairly soft mixture.

6. Whisk the egg whites until they form peaks and fold them carefully into the mixture.

7. Spread the mixture carefully onto the Swiss roll tin and bake it for 10-15 minutes until it rises and is firm to the touch.

8. Allow it to cool slightly and then place a clean, damp tea-towel over the top until absolutely cold.

9. Sprinkle a sheet of greaseproof paper generously with grated Parmesan. Loosen the edges of the roulade and tip it gently on to the paper.

10. Spread the roulade with mayonnaise and then lay the sliced mushrooms, onions and tomatoes on top. Season well and using the greaseproof paper, roll the roulade up as you would a Swiss roll. Lay it on a plate and garnish with chopped parsley. Serve the roulade cut into slices.

SUNBURST SALAD

Imperial (Metric)
2 medium-sized carrots
½ lb (¼ kilo) Cheddar cheese
½ cucumber
1 large lettuce
1 tablespoonful crunchy peanut
  butter
French dressing (page 13)

American
2 medium-sized carrots
2 cupsful grated Cheddar cheese
½ cucumber
1 large lettuce
1 tablespoonful crunchy peanut
  butter
French dressing (page 13)

1. Peel the carrots and grate them coarsely. Use the same grater for the cheese, then slice the cucumber thinly.

2. Line a salad bowl with lettuce leaves and arrange the grated cheese and carrots in alternate heaps around the bowl, with the cucumber slices in between. Beat the peanut butter into the French dressing, which will thicken considerably, and serve separately.

TANGY MIXED VEGETABLE SALAD

Imperial (Metric)	American
1 small carrot	1 small carrot
1 stick of celery	1 stick of celery
1 medium-sized onion	1 medium-sized onion
½ parsnip	½ parsnip
1 small tomato	1 small tomato
1 medium-sized apple	1 medium-sized apple
1 courgette	1 zucchini
1 leek	1 leek
2 sprigs of cauliflower	2 sprigs of cauliflower
A few capers	A few capers
2 green olives	2 green olives
½ teaspoonful lemon juice	½ teaspoonful lemon juice
2 teaspoonsful raw cane sugar	2 teaspoonsful raw cane sugar
Seasoning to taste	Seasoning to taste
2 tablespoonsful mayonnaise (page 14)	2½ tablespoonsful mayonnaise (page 14)
Parsley to garnish	Parsley to garnish

1. After washing the vegetables and apple, cut them into small cubes. Slice the leek and cauliflower finely, then chop the capers and olives.

2. Put all the vegetables into a deep bowl.

3. Pour over the lemon juice and sugar with the seasoning and then mix in the mayonnaise very carefully so as not to break up the vegetables. Garnish with the parsley.

TOMATOES FILLED WITH CREAM CHEESE

Imperial (Metric)	American
8 medium-sized, firm tomatoes	8 medium-sized, firm tomatoes
4 teaspoonsful mayonnaise (page 14)	4 teaspoonsful mayonnaise (page 14)
8 teaspoonsful cream cheese	8 teaspoonsful cream cheese
4 teaspoonsful milk or cream	4 teaspoonsful milk or cream
1 teaspoonful lemon juice	1 teaspoonful lemon juice
½ teaspoonful dried or fresh chopped dill	½ teaspoonful dried or fresh chopped dill
Seasoning to taste	Seasoning to taste
½ teaspoonful paprika	½ teaspoonful paprika
4 teaspoonsful chopped fresh parsley and chives, mixed	4 teaspoonsful chopped fresh parsley and chives, mixed

1. Cut the tops off the tomatoes and keep the tops as lids.

2. Scoop out the centres of the tomatoes and mix them well with all the other ingredients.

3. Use the mixture to fill the tomatoes and replace the tops. Decorate the tomatoes with the chopped parsley.

WHITE HARICOT BEAN SALAD

Imperial (Metric)
1 lb (½ kilo) cooked white haricot
  beans
8 spring onions
1 dessertspoonful chopped fresh
  parsley

American
2 cupsful cooked navy
  beans
8 scallions
1 tablespoonful chopped fresh
  parsley

Dressing:

Imperial (Metric)
5 tablespoonsful olive oil
1 tablespoonful tarragon vinegar
1 teaspoonful ready-made French
  mustard
½ teaspoonful raw cane sugar
Seasoning to taste

American
6 tablespoonsful olive oil
1 tablespoonful tarragon vinegar
1 teaspoonful ready-made French
  mustard
½ teaspoonful raw cane sugar
Seasoning to taste

1. Put the beans into a salad bowl then chop the spring onions and add them to the beans.

2. Mix the dressing ingredients thoroughly in a jam jar and pour it over salad. Toss the salad well.

3. Garnish with the fresh chopped parsley just before serving and chill the salad well.

WINTER SALAD

Imperial (Metric)
4 medium-sized potatoes, cooked
1 medium-sized onion
2 carrots
1 small, red eating apple
½ small white cabbage
2 sticks celery
2 pickled gherkins, chopped
Chopped fresh parsley
French dressing (page 13)

American
4 medium-sized potatoes, cooked
1 medium-sized onion
2 carrots
1 small, red eating apple
½ small white cabbage
2 sticks celery
2 pickled gherkins, chopped
Chopped fresh parsley
French dressing (page 13)

1. Dice the potatoes.

2. Peel and dice the onion, then peel and grate the carrots and grate the apple and cabbage.

3. Slice the celery finely.

4. Put all the ingredients into a bowl and pour the French dressing over them, combining well.

Note: This salad can be prepared and dressed in advance and left in the refrigerator.

4.

SALADS WITH FRUIT

ALMOND, AVOCADO AND PEAR SALAD

Imperial (Metric)	American
3 avocados	3 avocados
Juice of 1 lemon	Juice of 1 lemon
2 small dessert pears	2 small dessert pears
1/3 pint (200ml) sour cream	3/4 cupful sour cream
2 teaspoonsful tarragon vinegar	2 teaspoonful tarragon vinegar
1 teaspoonful French mustard	1 teaspoonful French mustard
1 teaspoonful raw cane sugar	1 teaspoonful raw cane sugar
Seasoning to taste	Seasoning to taste
3 tablespoonsful salted almonds	3½ tablespoonsful salted almonds
Toasted almond flakes	Toasted almond flakes
Chopped chives	Chopped chives

1. Cut the avocados in half, remove the stones, scoop out the flesh and save the shells. Dice the flesh, put it into a bowl and sprinkle with the lemon juice.

2. Peel, core and dice the dessert pears and put them with the avocados.

3. Make a dressing with the sour cream, tarragon vinegar, mustard and sugar. Season to taste.

4. Chop the almonds and add these to the pears. Pour the dressing over the top and mix it in gently.

5. Put the mixture into the avocado shells, cover them in cling film and chill well. Before serving, garnish the avocados with flaked almonds and chives.

AMERICAN SALAD

Imperial (Metric)	American
1 large orange	1 large orange
1 grapefruit	1 grapefruit
2 medium-sized apples	2 medium-sized apples
3 medium-sized tomatoes	3 medium-sized tomatoes
2 tablespoonsful apple juice	2½ tablespoonsful apple juice
1 teaspoonful raw cane sugar	1 teaspoonful raw cane sugar
Lettuce	Lettuce
1 tablespoonful whipped cream	1 tablespoonful whipped cream

1. Wash the fruit. Divide the orange and grapefruit into segments and halve each one. Chop the apples and tomatoes into approx. 1-in. chunks.

2. Mix the fruit and tomatoes together in a bowl and pour the apple juice and sugar over them.

3. Serve the salad piled on a bed of lettuce, topped with whipped cream.

APPLE AND DATE SALAD

Imperial (Metric)	American
3 medium-sized apples	3 medium-sized apples
16 stoned dates	16 stoned dates
3 teaspoonsful raw cane sugar	3 teaspoonsful raw cane sugar
3 teaspoonsful lemon juice	3 teaspoonsful lemon juice
3 tablespoonsful cream	3½ tablespoonsful cream
1 tablespoonful almond flakes	1 tablespoonful almond flakes

1. Wash the apples, cut them into quarters and then into thin slices.

2. Wash the dates and cut them into thin slices then put them in a bowl with the apples.

3. Mix together the sugar, lemon juice and cream and pour the dressing over the salad. Garnish with the almond flakes.

BEANSPROUT AND APPLE SALAD WITH COCONUT DRESSING

Imperial (Metric)	American
1 small green cabbage	1 small green cabbage
1 large apple	1 large apple
1 cupful beansprouts (alfalfa or mung)	1¼ cupsful beansprouts (alfalfa or mung)
4 tablespoonsful cider vinegar	5 tablespoonsful cider vinegar
4 tablespoonsful natural yogurt	5 tablespoonsful natural yogurt
1 oz (25g) unsweetened desiccated coconut	⅓ cupful unsweetened desiccated coconut
Pinch of sea salt	Pinch of sea salt
Toasted unsweetened desiccated coconut to garnish	Toasted unsweetened desiccated coconut to garnish

1. Shred the cabbage and apple finely and put them into a serving bowl with the beansprouts.

2. Make a dressing with the cider vinegar, yogurt, sugar, coconut and salt to taste.

3. Pour the dressing over the salad and mix it in well. Garnish with toasted desiccated coconut.

BEANSPROUT AND ORANGE SALAD

Imperial (Metric)
2 oranges
¼ head Chinese leaves
1 chicory
1 cupful beansprouts
1 red pepper

American
2 oranges
¼ head Chinese leaves
1 chicory
1¼ cupsful beansprouts
1 red pepper

Dressing:

Imperial (Metric)
2 tablespoonsful soy sauce
2 tablespoonsful lemon juice
1 tablespoonful sunflower oil
1 tablespoonful clear honey
1 teaspoonful ground ginger
Pinch of cayenne pepper
Toasted cashew nuts to garnish

American
2½ tablespoonsful soy sauce
2½ tablespoonsful lemon juice
1 tablespoonful sunflower oil
1 tablespoonful clear honey
1 teaspoonful ground ginger
Pinch of cayenne pepper
Toasted cashew nuts to garnish

1. Grate the orange rind finely, then remove and slice the flesh, removing the pips. Place the orange in a large bowl.

2. Cut the Chinese leaves finely and add them to the oranges.

3. Slice the chicory leaves in half crossways and add these and the beansprouts to the Chinese leaves and oranges.

4. Slice the red pepper crossways, removing the seeds and add this to the salad.

5. Combine all the dressing ingredients. Mix them thoroughly and pour the mixture over the salad. Garnish with toasted cashew nuts.

BEETROOT WITH APPLE

Imperial (Metric)	American
3 small, raw beetroots	3 small, raw beets
2 large cooking apples	2 large cooking apples
4 tablespoonsful sunflower oil	5 tablespoonsful sunflower oil
½ tablespoonful lemon juice	½ tablespoonful lemon juice
2 teaspoonsful raw cane sugar	2 teaspoonsful raw cane sugar

1. Peel the beetroot and grate it finely.

2. Wash the apples and grate them (include the peel).

3. Mix the apple and beetroot together in a deep bowl, then mix the oil, lemon juice and sugar together and pour the dressing over the salad, mixing it in thoroughly.

CARROT AND BANANA SALAD

Imperial (Metric)
3 medium-sized carrots
2 bananas
3 teaspoonsful lemon juice
3 tablespoonsful cream
3 teaspoonsful raw cane sugar
Chopped fresh parsley

American
3 medium-sized carrots
2 bananas
3 teaspoonsful lemon juice
3½ tablespoonsful cream
3 teaspoonsful raw cane sugar
Chopped fresh parsley

1. Wash and shred the carrots. Cut the bananas lengthwise and then into thin slices across.

2. Mix the lemon juice with the cream and sugar.

3. Put the banana and carrot into a serving bowl and pour the dressing over them. Mix the salad and garnish with the parsley.

CARROT WITH COCONUT SALAD

Imperial (Metric)
4 medium-sized carrots
1 tablespoonful pure orange juice
½ pint (¼ litre) thin cream
2 oz (50g) unsweetened desiccated
  coconut
1 tablespoonful raw cane sugar

American
4 medium-sized carrots
1 tablespoonful pure orange juice
1⅓ cupsful thin cream
⅔ cupful unsweetened desiccated
  coconut
1 tablespoonful raw cane sugar

1. Peel and grate the carrot and place it in a bowl.

2. Add the orange juice to the cream gradually so as not to curdle it
   and whisk well. Add the coconut and sugar and whisk again
   well. Pour the dressing over the grated carrot.

COCONUT, CARROT AND RAISIN SALAD

Imperial (Metric)	American
½ lb (¼ kilo) carrots	½ lb carrots
2 oz (50g) raisins	⅓ cupful raisins
¼ pint (150ml) pure orange juice	⅔ cupful pure orange juice
2 oz (50g) unsweetened desiccated coconut	⅔ cupful unsweetened desiccated coconut

1. Grate the carrots.

2. Gently cook the raisins in orange juice to swell them, then leave them to cool.

3. Mix the carrot, coconut, raisins and orange juice in a bowl and chill the salad well before serving.

DRIED FRUIT SALAD

Imperial (Metric)	American
1 lb 2 oz (650g) dried prunes	3¼ cupsful dried prunes
9 oz (250g) dried apricots	2 cupsful dried apricots
1 oz (25g) fresh ginger	1 oz fresh ginger
Clear honey	Clear honey
1 teaspoonful lemon juice	1 teaspoonful lemon juice
1 tablespoonful chopped nuts	1 tablespoonful chopped nuts

1. Soak the prunes and apricots overnight.

2. Chop the ginger finely.

3. Cook the prunes, apricots and ginger for an hour and sweeten them to taste with the honey.

4. Allow the salad to chill for at least a day.

5. Before serving, add the lemon juice and garnish with the chopped nuts. Serve with natural yogurt.

FRUITY BEANSPROUT SALAD

Imperial (Metric)	American
2 apples	2 apples
2 bananas	2 bananas
4 oz (100g) beansprouts	2 cupsful beansprouts
2 oz (50g) raisins	⅓ cupful raisins
2 oz (50g) sunflower seeds	½ cupful sunflower seeds
¼ pint (150ml) natural yogurt	⅔ cupful natural yogurt
Clear honey to sweeten	Clear honey to sweeten
1 oz (25g) toasted wheatgerm	¼ cupful toasted wheatgerm

1. Grate the apples, including the skins and slice the bananas finely.

2. Put the washed and dried sprouts into a bowl and mix in the apple, banana, raisins and sunflower seeds.

3. Pour the yogurt over the salad and mix it in well. Sweeten with honey if required and sprinkle with the toasted wheatgerm.

Note: This can be served as an unusual and invigorating breakfast dish.

GRAPE SALAD

Imperial (Metric)	American
½ lb (¼ kilo) ripe grapes	½ lb ripe grapes
2 apples	2 apples
2 oranges	2 oranges
2 or 3 fresh cherries	2 or 3 fresh cherries
1 tablespoonful apple juice	1 tablespoonful apple juice
1 tablespoonful raw cane sugar	1 tablespoonful raw cane sugar
Lettuce	Lettuce
1 tablespoonful whipped cream	1 tablespoonful whipped cream
2 teaspoonsful flaked almonds	2 teaspoonsful flaked almonds

1. Wash the grapes, drain them and cut each one in half and remove pips.

2. Slice the apples and cut them into 1-in. chunks. Peel and divide the orange into segments and then chop each segment in half. Cut the cherries in half and remove the stones.

3. Mix all the fruit together with the apple juice, sugar and some water. Serve the salad on a bed of lettuce topped with cream and flaked almonds.

KIWI FRUIT SALAD

Imperial (Metric)
5 kiwi fruit
1 lb (1½ kilo) tomatoes
1 cupful chopped fresh mint

American
5 kiwi fruit
1 lb tomatoes
1¼ cupsful chopped fresh mint

Dressing:

Imperial (Metric)
1 tablespoonful cider vinegar
3 tablespoonsful sunflower oil
¼ teaspoonful raw cane sugar
Seasoning to taste

American
1 tablespoonful cider vinegar
3½ tablespoonsful sunflower oil
¼ teaspoonful raw cane sugar
Seasoning to taste

1. Peel the kiwi fruit carefully and slice them across thinly.

2. Slice the tomatoes into rounds and lay the slices on a serving dish, alternating each slice with one of kiwi fruit, slightly overlapping.

3. Mix the dressing ingredients thoroughly and pour over the tomatoes and kiwi fruit. Garnish the salad with the chopped mint and chill before serving.

ORANGE AND CHICORY SALAD

Imperial (Metric)	American
3 oranges	3 oranges
4 heads of celery	4 heads of celery
6 tablespoonful olive oil	7½ tablespoonful olive oil
Seasoning to taste	Seasoning to taste
2 tablespoonful pure orange juice	2 tablespoonful pure orange juice

1. Peel, de-pith and slice the oranges into thin segments.

2. Wash the chicory and cut it crossways into slices ¼ in. thick.

3. Combine the olive oil, seasoning and orange juice and pour the dressing over the salad.

4. Toss the salad gently and serve it immediately.

PEAR AND GRAPE SALAD

Imperial (Metric)	American
Head of lettuce	Head of lettuce
4 ripe pears	4 ripe pears
6 oz (150g) cream cheese	¾ cupful cream cheese
3 tablespoonsful mayonnaise (page 14)	3 tablespoonsful mayonnaise (page 14)
Sea salt and freshly ground black pepper	Sea salt and freshly ground black pepper
½ lb (¼ kilo) green grapes	½ lb green grapes

1. Wash and dry the lettuce leaves and arrange them on a serving plate.

2. Peel then halve and core the pears. Place the cut halves downwards.

3. Mix the cheese and mayonnaise thoroughly. Season well and carefully spread the mixture over the pears.

4. Skin, halve and de-pip the grapes and press them firmly on the cheese-covered pears.

5. Arrange the pears on the serving plate. Chill well before serving.

PEARS WITH CREAM CHEESE BALLS

Imperial (Metric)
3 oz (75g) flaked almonds
½ lb (¼ kilo) cream cheese
4 ripe pears
Juice of 1 lemon
1 lettuce
Chopped fresh parsley

American
¾ cupful flaked almonds
1 cupful cream cheese
4 ripe pears
Juice of 1 lemon
1 lettuce
Chopped fresh parsley

Dressing:

Imperial (Metric)
4 tablespoonsful mayonnaise
   (page 14)
1 tablespoonful tomato purée
1 tablespoonful cream
Dash of Tabasco sauce
Dash of vegetarian Worcester sauce
   (Holbrook's)
Seasoning to taste

American
5 tablespoonsful mayonnaise
   (page 14)
1 tablespoonful tomato purée
1 tablespoonful cream
Dash of Tabasco sauce
Dash of vegetarian Worcester sauce
   (Holbrook's)
Seasoning to taste

1. Chop and toast the almonds.

2. Roll the cream cheese into small balls and roll them in the toasted nuts, then chill well.

3. Peel, core and halve the pears, then dip them in lemon juice to prevent them discolouring.

4. Mix together the mayonnaise, *purée*, cream, Tabasco, Worcester sauce and seasoning.

5. Arrange the outer lettuce leaves on a serving plate. Quarter the heart and arrange it in the centre. Pile the cheese balls on the pears and lay them on the dish. Add the dressing and garnish with parsley.

PUMPKIN WITH APPLE SALAD

Imperial (Metric)
½ lb (¼ kilo) pumpkin, peeled
2 medium-sized cooking apples
3 tablespoonsful cream
3 teaspoonsful lemon juice
2 teaspoonsful raw cane sugar
4 teaspoonsful grated nuts

American
½ lb pumpkin, peeled
2 medium-sized cooking apples
3½ tablespoonsful cream
3 teaspoonsful lemon juice
2 teaspoonsful raw cane sugar
4 teaspoonsful grated nuts

1. Shred the pumpkin on a coarse grater and grate the apples finely.

2. Make a dressing of the cream, lemon juice and sugar. Mix this dressing in a large bowl with the apple and pumpkin and top with the grated nuts.

SPECIAL SUMMER SALAD

Imperial (Metric)	American
1 pineapple	1 pineapple
1 banana	1 banana
6 apricots	6 apricots
½ melon	½ melon
6 oz (150g) grapes	6 oz grapes
4 oz (100g) shredded unsweetened coconut	1⅓ cupsful shredded unsweetened coconut
1 pint (½ litre) sour cream	2½ cupsful sour cream
1 oz (25g) chopped walnuts	¼ cupful chopped English walnuts

1. Chill the pineapple well, slice it in half, cut out the core and then dice it.

2. Cut up the banana, apricots and melon. Halve the grapes and de-pip them.

3. Put all the fruit into a bowl and add the coconut.

4. Pour over the sour cream and garnish with the chopped walnuts. Chill well before serving.

STRAWBERRY AND CUCUMBER SALAD

Imperial (Metric)
1 small cucumber
12 large strawberries
2 tablespoonsful white wine
  vinegar
Seasoning to taste

American
1 small cucumber
12 large strawberries
2½ tablespoonsful white wine
  vinegar
Seasoning to taste

1. Peel the cucumber and slice it finely.

2. Wash and hull the strawberries, drain them well and cut them into even slices.

3. Arrange the slices on a serving plate, first an outer circle of cucumber slices, then a slightly overlapping circle of strawberries, and so on, finishing with a central circle of strawberry slices.

4. Sprinkle with white wine vinegar, season lightly and chill well before serving.

SWEET AND SOUR SALAD

Imperial (Metric)	American
1 medium-sized grapefruit	1 medium-sized grapefruit
4 medium-sized eating apples	4 medium-sized eating apples
3 oz (75g) fresh pineapple	3 oz fresh pineapple
2 heads of chicory	2 heads of chicory
1 pickled cucumber	1 pickled cucumber
Finely chopped fresh mint	Finely chopped fresh mint

Dressing:

Imperial (Metric)	American
1 tablespoonful lemon juice	1 tablespoonful lemon juice
1 tablespoonful clear honey	1 tablespoonful clear honey
2 tablespoonsful sunflower oil	2½ tablespoonsful sunflower oil
1 tablespoonful cider vinegar	1 tablespoonful cider vinegar
1 teaspoonful sea salt	1 teaspoonful sea salt
Freshly ground black pepper	Freshly ground black pepper
Grated rind of ½ orange	Grated rind of ½ orange

1. Peel, core and dice the grapefruit and apples. Cube the pineapple.

2. Slice the chicory finely, chop the cucumber and place the vegetables in a salad bowl.

3. Mix the dressing ingredients in a jam jar and shake them well. Pour the mixture over the salad, toss it well and chill it for about an hour.

4. Garnish with the chopped mint before serving.

TANGY AVOCADO

Imperial (Metric)	American
3 large avocado pears	3 large avocado pears
Juice of 1 small lemon	Juice of 1 small lemon
1 large orange	1 large orange
1 large grapefruit	1 large grapefruit
Fresh mint to garnish	Fresh mint to garnish

1. Peel the avocados, then quarter them and remove the stones. Slice the avocados into thin sections and sprinkle them with lemon juice.

2. Peel the orange and the grapefruit, carefully retaining any juice, and slice them into segments. Place the fruit in a large bowl and pour any juice over them.

3. Carefully mix the avocado with the orange and grapefruit. Spoon the salad into individual dishes and garnish with the fresh mint.

TROPICAL MANGO SALAD

Imperial (Metric)	American
1½ cupsful sliced ripe mango	2 cupsful sliced ripe mango
1 cupful sliced, peeled and de-seeded orange	1¼ cupsful sliced, peeled and de-seeded orange
Juice of 1 large lime	Juice of 1 large lime
2 tablespoonsful clear honey	2 tablespoonsful clear honey
5 tablespoonsful sunflower oil	6 tablespoonsful sunflower oil
Pinch of sea salt	Pinch of sea salt
4 crisp lettuce leaves	4 crisp lettuce leaves
6 maraschino cherries	6 maraschino cherries

1. Put the fruit into a bowl and mix it gently.

2. Make a dressing with the lime juice, honey, oil and salt. Pour the dressing over the fruit and mix it gently. Chill well.

3. To serve, put equal amounts of salad into four bowls lined with the lettuce leaves. Garnish with the maraschino cherries.

WALDORF SALAD

Imperial (Metric)
2 tablespoonsful lemon juice
1 teaspoonful raw cane sugar
1 lb (½ kilo) eating apples
¼ pint (150ml) mayonnaise
  (page 14)
2 oz (50g) shelled walnuts
½ head of celery
1 lettuce

American
2½ tablespoonsful lemon juice
1 teaspoonful raw cane sugar
1 lb eating apples
⅔ cupful mayonnaise
  (page 14)
¼ cupful shelled English walnuts
½ head of celery
1 lettuce

1. Place the lemon juice and sugar in a large bowl and mix them thoroughly.

2. Reserving one apple for garnishing, core and dice the remaining apples and put them into the bowl with the lemon juice and sugar. Mix the ingredients well and add the mayonnaise.

3. Chop the walnuts and celery and add them to the apple and mayonnaise mixture, combining them thoroughly.

4. Separate the lettuce leaves and wash them well, then line a serving bowl with them. Core and slice the remaining apple and sprinkle it with lemon juice to prevent discoloration.

5. Put the apples, celery, walnuts and mayonnaise into the serving bowl and garnish the salad with the slices of apple.

INDEX